Wisdom With Understanding is Better Than Rubies

Lurine Karon Greenberg
Fine Arts Collection

Mary Emmerling's
Romantic Country

Mary Emmerling's Romantic Country

Style That's Straight from the Heart

Text by Jill Kirchner Simpson
Photographs by Michael Skott

Clarkson Potter/Publishers
New York

Published by Clarkson Potter/Publishers, New York, New York.
Member of the Crown Publishing Group, a division of Random House, Inc.
www.randomhouse.com

CLARKSON N. POTTER is a trademark and POTTER and colophon are registered
trademarks of Random House, Inc.

Printed in China

Design by Felicity Keane

Library of Congress Cataloging-in-Publication
Emmerling, Mary.
    Mary Emmerling's romantic country : style that's straight from the heart /
by Mary Emmerling ; text by Jill Kirchner Simpson ; photographs by Michael Skott.
    1. Interior decoration—Psychological aspects.   I. Title: Romantic country.
II. Kirchner, Jill.   III. Skott, Michael.   IV. Title.
    NK2113.E47   2003
    747' .01'9—dc21   2003009909

ISBN 0-609-61009-0

10   9   8   7   6   5   4   3   2

To

August 13, 1996 — when I met Reg Jackson

September 15, 2002 — when my son, Jonathan Emmerling, and Betsy McCall moved in together

September 13, 2003 — when my daughter, Samantha Emmerling, and Sam Henning were married

South Mars 1 1820

Pardevant Pierre Pennier
Notaire ... à Mouy en Beauvoisis
Soussigné ... en présence des témoins cy après nommez

Fut présent Besnoist Poullain laboureur demeurant à
Saint Félix étant ce jour à Mouy

Lequel à par ces présentes vendu cédé quitté et délaissé
promis et s'oblige garantir de touts troubles et empêchemens
généralement quelconques dès maintenant et à toujours

À Félix Pommery le jeune talonnier demeurant à
Cailloux paroisse de Harinck étant aussi ce jour audit
Mouy à ce présent et acceptant acquéreur pour lui ses hoirs
et ayans causes

Premièrement Dix huit verges de terre sisck au
terroir de fay Souk le Bois tandu la rue de Selles
soignantes d'un coté à Jean Louis Dubus, d'autre coté
à Thomas Gérin d'un bout à plusieurs, et d'autre bout
au chemin

Item Dix huit autres verges de terre au même lieu
tenantes d'un coté à la veuve Lucien Pommery, d'autre coté
audit Gérin, d'un bout audit chemin, et d'autre bout au
jardin de la veuve Charles Bitre un pied sente entre de

ACKNOWLEDGMENTS

First, I want to thank Reg Jackson for making *every* day special and romantic.

How can I ever thank all my friends after twenty books? Each and every one of you has never turned me down, generously inviting me into your lives and sharing your friends. Thanks especially to Carol and Mark Glasser, who have always opened up their hearts and home to me, when I've been in love and out; to Beverly Jacomini, who has been a blessed friend from the first American Country book (oh, those romantic nights at the farm with full moons and Tommy's margaritas!); and to Ann Lawrence, for opening new doors to romantic decorating.

Thanks always to my brother, Terry Ellisor, who now owns the most romantic restaurant in Scottsdale, Arizona, the Zinc Bistro (maybe you will fall in love, too?), and my children, Samantha Emmerling and Jonathan Emmerling, who know how to be romantic in their own lives and are now having fun decorating their own apartments with romantic touches. And to my new family: Devin Thompson and family, and Mishawn Roggeman and family.

I can't do a wonderful book without Michael Skott, my photographer, who has that magic touch with the light and the camera; Felicity Keane, who understood my vision of romance without all the lace and fluff, and designed this beautiful book; and Jill Kirchner Simpson, who helped me say what I wanted to say in just the right way.

There would be no *Romantic Country* without the following friends who shared their fabulous homes with us. Each and every one has their own creative definition of romantic decorating: Penni Oliver and Jean Bown, Peri Wolfman and Charley Gold, Paula and Gordon Hamilton, Nancy and Michael Weber, Kim and Bruce Fiscus, Mary and Mike Mulcahy, Jean and Pat Brooks, Kay O'Toole, Thomas and Claire Callaway, Carol and Mark Glasser, Donna Temple Brown, Pamela and Bob Melet, Jolie Kelter and Michael Malcé, Beverly and Tommy Jacomini, Gloria List, Dianne Cash, Karin Blake, Mary Porter, Brian and Kathi Stinger, Nancy and Jack Lacy, and Georgia Bates.

To Gayle Benderoff and Deborah Geltman, still my fabulous agents, who know a good idea when they see one. Annetta Hanna, my great new editor at Clarkson Potter, as well as Marysarah Quinn, Maggie Hinders, Joan Denman, and Sibylle Kazeroid. Carol Sama Sheehan, Jen Kopf Zimmerman (and special love to the memory and spirit of Paul Zimmerman), and the wonderful staff at *Country Home* magazine.

Sue Balmforth at Bountiful, a friend who has not only opened so many doors for me but also knew Reg well before I did.

And to Lyn Hutchings, who in July 1996 gave me a Carol Anthony painting that said "New Beginnings" . . . and then three weeks later it all happened.

If all this book does is make you think about lighting a candle, buying yourself flowers, opening up a bottle of wine with dinner, or indulging in beautiful bed linens, then I am happy that we made your day a little more special. To sparklers and champagne!

CONTENTS

INTRODUCTION

Writing *Romantic Country* at this time in my life has a very special resonance for me because of an amazing story I want to share with you.

I often feel like I have lived three lives. I spent ten years married to a wonderful man with whom I had my terrific children, Samantha and Jonathan. I then spent ten years with a photographer, traveling all over the world, writing my books, working for magazines, and living a great adventure. After we broke up, I lived through the worst six months of my life. My mother died, my magazine folded, and I was on my own. Sometimes you just get to a point in your life where you realize you need to make some changes: I decided to leave New York and start over. I had just bought a little house in Santa Fe. (Every time I come out West, I feel like it's in my blood—I just love it here.) So one day in the middle of a blizzard, I filled my car with some of my favorite antiques, a stack of magazines, and pots of orchids, and drove for four days. I stayed at Holiday Inn

Expresses, smoked cigarettes (I never smoke), listened to Spanish language tapes, and drove straight through to Santa Fe.

Over the winter I did something I had never done before: I spoke with an amazing psychic, Debra Ritchey, in Fort Worth, Texas. Friends had raved about her and urged me to call. I figured, my friends are sick of listening to me, I'm sick of listening to myself, what can it hurt? She told me many things that proved to be true, and she also said, "You can't rush things, but I see you meeting someone with dark hair (with a little bit of gray) between June and September. He'll tell you, 'I know you've been hurt before, but I'm going to prove to you that not all men are like that.'"

I spent time over the summer in my new home in Santa Fe, and in August, I photographed it for *Ladies' Home Journal.* One night, my friends and I had a reservation at Café Pasqual, but we were running late and the hostess gave away our table. We went to Coyote Cantina instead to have a margarita and watch the sunset, and even changed tables a couple of times to get a better view. My friend and editor Kimberlie Waugh was asking me what kind of man I would want to meet, and I said, "Someone like that guy over there in the cowboy hat with the cute butt!" That man, Reg Jackson, happened to look over at that very moment, and we all burst into giggles because we thought he had heard me. He came over and asked what we were laughing about and we started talking—he was in the art business and was in Santa Fe for Indian Market. We went on together to another spot to go dancing—Reg is the best dancer you've ever seen. An older woman came up to us and said, "You two are so cute together; how long have you been married?"

When we told her we had just met, she said, "You two will be together for the rest of your lives!" And we've been together ever since. What's most amazing, however, is that Reg actually said to me that night, "You have this look in your eyes like you've been hurt before, and maybe you don't trust men anymore, but I'm going to prove you wrong." I kicked Kimberlie under the table when he said that, because she knew what the psychic had told me!

Shortly after Reg and I met, I left for a three-week trip to Africa and told him he could stay at my house. I began to wonder if I was crazy to do that, but it turns out that when Reg saw my closet, and that we had almost an identical wardrobe of flannel shirts, fringed leather jackets, and cowboy boots, he fell in love. One day shortly after I got back Reg said to me, "There's something I have to tell you," and I thought, "Oh no, here it comes." And he said, "I have nine grandchildren!" With a huge sigh of relief, I said, "That's great, as long as they don't call me Grandma!" So now I have nine kids calling me "Graham Cracker"!

At that point in my life, I figured I didn't really need to get married again, but when we had been together a year and a half, Reg came to me with a beautiful canary diamond and asked me to marry him. We've now been married more than five years, and on our fifth anniversary, we got Cinco, our dog.

I feel so incredibly fortunate. Reg and I have both been through enough that we know life is too precious to waste time fighting. We live in different cities—me in Des Moines for my work as creative director of *Country Home* magazine, and Reg in Phoenix for his work—but we meet on the weekends, in our little house in Santa Fe (which you'll see in this book), or in Phoenix, or wherever I'm traveling for work. While it is kind of a crazy life, it keeps the romance alive. Being together is more important than anything, and we know that if we were together all the time, we would be happy, too. Finding such wonderful love a little later in life, we never take it for granted. We send each other love notes (not e-mail!), I buy fresh flowers and light candles, we have champagne for no occasion at all.

When Reg entered my life, the word *romance* took on a whole new meaning. I had thought I would never have another big romance in my life, and actually, that was fine with me. Especially for women, it's your girlfriends who are really there for you anyway, who sustain you. When life goes to hell and back, your girlfriends help you through bad times and share in the good times.

That's why romantic decorating for me is not just about being part of a couple, or putting lace on the bed (for one thing, most men aren't that crazy about lace!). "Romantic" can mean heirlooms that connect you to your past, tokens of affection from your children or friends, treasured collections, mementos from a wonderful trip—in short, anything that has meaning to you, that tugs at your heartstrings ever so softly every time you see it. It's decorating based on what resonates for *you*, not what's in all the latest magazines. In this book, I'll take you to homes of couples, single women, women living on their own after a divorce, young families with kids, and "empty nesters"; homes where men have done the decorating, ones where it's totally the woman's passion, and those in which it's truly a joint effort. A romantic home simply means one where you feel nurtured, pampered, and soothed; one

where you enjoy entertaining and being with friends; and where you can also enjoy being alone, because we all need the replenishing peace of solitude.

I'm not really a "lace and frills" kind of person, and I don't believe in defining romance that narrowly. To me, a fire burning in a kiva in Santa Fe is romantic; the respite of a lush garden terrace in Houston's heat is romantic; a charming collection of silver dachshunds because you adore your dogs is romantic; the soul-stirring spectacle of the American flag is romantic. All-white is undoubtedly romantic, but so are Tuscan yellows, flattering apricots, fiery reds, and brilliant sky blues, if they're what you love. Wear your heart on your sleeve when you decorate: Let visitors feel like a little bit of your soul has been revealed and shared with them when they're invited into your home. What's romantic is intensely personal and idiosyncratic: It should be different for each person, just as our passions, loves, and pursuits are all different. For a shy romantic, the surprise of a staid cabinet's lush red interior or just a few vintage floral pillows tucked on neutral sofas and chairs might do the trick; for a sensualist, touchable textures like velvet, chenille, fur, or cashmere spell seduction. For almost all of us, candlelight, a fire in the fireplace, and a bouquet of full-blown fresh flowers are timelessly romantic.

In our increasingly hard-edged, fast-paced, technology-ruled times, it seems to me that romance is more important than ever. Taking refuge in sensory pleasures and surrounding yourself with tactile and visual antidotes has become all the more essential. I hope this book will inspire you, no matter who you are or where you live, to put a little more romance in your life!

Cabbage roses, whitewashed flea-market furniture, wrought-iron beds, faded vintage floral fabrics . . . cottage romance is all about easy charm, simple pleasures, and unabashed femininity. It's all in the mix: sparkling crystal chandeliers with timeworn painted pieces; chipped floral china with precious family heirlooms. Unify and update mismatched pieces with white paint and slipcovers, then add in lots of personal touches.

ABOVE: *A monogrammed lace tablecloth becomes a feminine slipcover on a club chair in the bedroom. The tiniest crystal chandelier and wide-slatted plantation shutters turn this alcove into a special sanctuary, the perfect place to curl up with a good book.*
RIGHT: *Small shades and a linen sleeve (concealing the chain) add polish to a dripping-with-charm chandelier in the dining room.*

Cottage Romance

WHITE MAGIC

*T*ucked away in a somewhat scruffy neighborhood in West Los Angeles is an amazing oasis of airy white charm. Enclosed in a garden brimming over with roses and bougainvillea, this tiny California bungalow from the 1930s seems like an enchanted cottage happened upon in a forbidding fairy-tale forest. Indoors and out, white is the rule in furnishings forgivingly slipcovered in Marseilles spreads, peeling-paint cupboards, wicker settees, and sheer, floor-skimming curtains that dance in the breeze. And yet, this is also the cottage its owners call "the house that doesn't matter"—reflecting their philosophy that scratches, spills, and stains simply aren't worth fretting over. The worn finishes, genuinely acquired patina of age, and washable slipcovers ensure that no one drip or tear is likely to stand out. The style is "comfy casual," says Penni Oliver, who owns the house with Jean Bown.

Both Penni and Jean worked at a wondrous Venice, California, store called Bountiful, which embodies their style. After a yearlong house hunt in Los Angeles's stratospheric real estate market, they had grown discouraged about the prospect of finding something affordable with charm. Then one day a customer told them she was selling her house, and it was love at first sight. The bonus of buying from someone with similar taste was that the house didn't need any work (as the sales flyer said, "Just bring your toothbrush!"). On buying trips for the store, they had occasionally put aside finds for their dream home, and once they bought the house, "we cherry-picked everything else we needed from Bountiful," says Penni. "Except for the stove and refrigerator, everything in this house is old."

The look is white, light, and clean, with icons of romance in abundance: airy wrought-iron beds, candles and fresh flowers everywhere (a fringe benefit of their devotion to the garden), the shimmer of mercury glass and crystal chandeliers, touches of vintage florals on throw pillows and curtains, and reminders of the nearby sea in bleached white starfish and shells. The existing wainscoting, French doors, and plantation shutters imbue the house with a vintage charm that's amplified by a few thoughtful additions, such as the gracious corner cupboard with a swirly pediment in the dining room. Though the house is a diminutive 1,200 square feet, the consistent, calming palette and the way the interior opens up to the outdoors make it feel spacious and serene. Penni and Jean may call it "the house that doesn't matter," but any visitor can see that it clearly does.

An easygoing mix of cushioned wicker chairs and side chairs with ruffled skirts gathers around an old leather-topped card table. A compact table like this, with leaves for expansion, and the corner cupboard are great space savers.

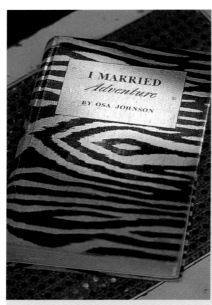  

ROMANTIC READS

THE CLASSICS

Some of the classics that have shaped our vision of love and passion:

Anna Karenina by Leo Tolstoy
Brideshead Revisited by Evelyn Waugh
For Whom the Bell Tolls by Ernest Hemingway
Gone With the Wind by Margaret Mitchell
Jane Eyre by Charlotte Brontë
Pride and Prejudice by Jane Austen
Lady Chatterley's Lover by D. H. Lawrence
Wuthering Heights by Emily Brontë

CONTEMPORARY FAVORITES

Great love stories to get lost in:

Atonement by Ian McEwan
Corelli's Mandolin by Louis De Bernieres
The English Patient by Michael Ondaatje
Girl with a Pearl Earring by Tracy Chevalier
The Last Time They Met by Anita Shreve
Memoirs of a Geisha by Arthur S. Golden
Possession by A. S. Byatt
The Remains of the Day by Kazuo Ishiguro

ABOVE: *Romantic touches in the bedroom—the zebra-striped* I Married Adventure, *Penni's vintage-lace lampshades, and an urn overflowing with flowers.*
RIGHT: *A medical cabinet, fitted with glass shelves and stocked with soaps, lotions, bleached starfish, and shells, adds beauty to the bath.*
FOLLOWING PAGES, CLOCKWISE FROM TOP LEFT: *Perfume bottles, lilies, and a vintage photograph compose a nostalgic dresser-top tableau. The old farm table, cut down to form a coffee table in the living room, was a gift from Sue Balmforth of Bountiful. Mercury glass on the mantel reflects the creamy glow of candlelight. Chenille and Marseilles spreads and lace-edged linens romance the bed.*

The look is white, *light,* and clean, with *icons* of

romance in abundance and *fresh flowers.*

Isn't It Romantic?

Roses cut fresh from the garden

A white lace tablecloth made into a slipcover

Lace-covered lampshades and
vintage sconces

Airy white linen curtains that graze the floor

Calla lilies mixed with pale peach tulips

The gleam of silver mercury glass in candlelight

Vintage perfume bottles collected on a bureau

Evocative reminders of the beach in every room

An antique urn planted with flowers
at the foot of the bed

French doors in the bedroom opening up
to a terrace planted with fragrant flowers

Flirtatious short gathered skirts on dining chairs

Flower paintings framed with
old barn boards

The light-catching sparkle of crystal
chandeliers, glass bottles, and vases

RIGHT AND FAR RIGHT: *The house is always*
filled with flowers, like these pale pink roses,
from Jean and Penni's garden.

THE BEST OF BOTH WORLDS

*T*he setting, in one of New York's popular summer communities on Long Island's South Shore, is idyllic: A classic shingle-style house from the 1890s nestled beside an apple orchard and a mere hop, skip, and jump from picturesque Mecox Bay, with the beach and Atlantic Ocean just beyond. "We can hear the ocean and smell the salt air from our windows, yet we're bordered by apple trees instead of houses," says Nancy Weber, a creative director for magazines, who with her husband, Michael, spends nearly every weekend at this much-loved escape from the pressures of life and work in Manhattan.

The turn-of-the-century house felt dark and claustrophobic when the Webers first bought it seven years ago. To open it up to the light without drastically altering its character, Nancy employed gestures both dramatic—installing a bank of windows and French doors opening onto a back deck—and simple—taking down the heavy curtains obscuring every window, uprooting the hedges that blocked the sun in the living room, and hanging mirrors opposite windows to reflect even more light. The Webers combined the existing kitchen and mudroom to expand the sense of space: A generous room encompassing a kitchen, an informal dining area, and a sunporch is now bathed in light.

When painting the rooms, Nancy took her cues from the views outside the windows, choosing shades with a hint of green from the trees, blue from the sea, and sand tones from the beach, as well as plenty of crisp white for the trim and beadboard. Scouting flea markets and antiques shows turned up cozy dark rattan furniture leavened with white cotton cushions, pillows fashioned from romantic vintage floral fabrics, peeling-paint wicker, and colorful Windsor chairs around a checkerboard-topped table. These finds give the home its warm, approachable character and help blend the new additions with the old. Sea-grass carpets throughout the house lend a consistent neutral backdrop, which gives a nice flow to the series of small rooms, as well as a beach-house casualness.

Nancy's favorite spot is the deck outside the kitchen. "I love to read and we often eat out there. It feels very private, sheltered by the apple trees with the soothing sound of the ocean." And when the Webers are inside, they open all the windows and doors: "I just want to feel like I'm immersed in that environment," Nancy says. "This house has all the charm of an old house, yet it feels open and light, and that's what we love about it."

RIGHT: *In a large central sitting/dining room, white-painted furniture sets off grand gestures like a wire basket of pears and tall, candlelit hurricanes.*
FOLLOWING PAGES: *The Webers stripped the living room's pine mantel to a honeyed glow. The fabric on a tag-sale chair serendipitously matched their sofa.*

Isn't It Romantic?

Lots of white paint and fabric, used to refresh old, dark furnishings

Dark rattan furniture for contrast and a Casablanca sense of sultry romance

Pond yachts, lanterns, fish, and other subtle reminders of the seaside setting

Old painted wicker furniture refreshed with gingham cushions

Walls with a blush of color

An unobtrusive pool ringed with hydrangeas, nestled beside a beautiful apple orchard

A hammock—always an invitation to lie down and lounge

Pillows fashioned from vintage fabric—florals, sailboat motifs, ticking stripes—for touches of softly

RIGHT: *A pale rainbow of Windsor chairs gathers around a painted checkerboard table in the kitchen. Here, wooden floors, dark in the rest of the house, are pickled for airy lightness. A pitcher of hydrangeas is one of summer's fringe benefits.*
FAR RIGHT: *The natural textures of rattan furniture and sea-grass carpets add important contrast to white furnishings in the sitting room. Sconces with floral fabric shades are a space-saving source of light.*

ROMANTIC BY NATURE

Here's romance that's free for the taking:

Thunderstorms

Snow days, and snowy walks at night

Stargazing

Spring rains

Skinny-dipping

Mountaintops

Waterfalls

Birds' nests

Sunsets

Beaches and oceans

Moonlight

Fireflies

Shooting stars and meteor showers

Letting the sun dry your skin

Staying up all night and watching the sun rise

Outdoor showers

LEFT, TOP: *Wrought-iron and rattan furnishings are open, airy choices for a beach house.* LEFT, BOTTOM: *The simple pool and surround let the stunning setting, framed by hydrangeas and the apple orchard, steal the show.* ABOVE: *In the sunporch off the kitchen, white beadboard, pickled floors, and white wicker furniture keep everything light and fresh.*

WEEKEND BLISS

*F*or years, Peri Wolfman and Charley Gold have been spending weekends in the Hamptons, a welcome respite from their fast-paced lives in New York City. In every house they have owned or rented, and in their SoHo loft as well, there have always been certain constants: open shelving and white marble counters in the kitchen; crisp white slipcovers contrasted with peeling-paint furniture; wonderful, eclectic collections, yet an overall impression of impeccable order and clean simplicity. As in the well-loved store they once owned in Manhattan, Wolfman-Gold, nearly everything is white, and there is a pleasing order and symmetry of repetition throughout. In Peri's world, if one is good, a half dozen are even better.

Their most recent Hamptons home is a seventeen-year-old red farmhouse that gives the impression of being much older than its years. Ringed by huge blue spruces and framed by a brilliant blue ruff of hydrangeas come August, the house "wraps its arms around you and gives you a hug," says Charley warmly. They spend winter nights curled up in the wood-paneled den by the fire, and in summer "the glider on the front porch is my coveted spot," Peri says. Though the house was filled with color and wallpaper when they bought it, they stripped it down to its bones and then just painted and added new hard-

ware. In the kitchen Peri and Charley ripped out the cabinetry, put in their signature open shelves, and added new appliances. The built-in shelves and cabinets were already in place in the living room; they just changed the hardware from shiny brass to a more rustic black iron that weathers the salt air well. When their copious collections of tableware (Peri oversees product design at Williams-Sonoma) wouldn't all fit in the kitchen, Charley started arranging the transferware plates and white ironstone pitchers on the living room bookcases. Peri applauded the move because "I have such a passion for tableware, I love to see it all the time"—hence her love of open shelving in the kitchen.

Peri and Charley are prolific entertainers, often having friends over for dinner two or more times a week. "It works because Charley is the cook," says Peri. "I couldn't do it alone. With women, everything has to be perfect, and we get uptight. To Charley, it's an enjoyment. I just set the table and do whatever he tells me to do." The size of their dining tables—indoors and out—attests to their love of feeding a crowd. The antique table in the dining room was paired with worn green chairs in a former house, but here Peri refreshed it with the counterpoint of crisp white slipcovered chairs from the budget-friendly West Elm catalog. A single-

An effortless summer centerpiece: garden blooms
and an all-American cluster of flags.

file series of simple white vases filled with late-summer sunflowers has much more impact than an individual centerpiece. The generous swoops of the iron chandelier, custom-forged by artisan John Battle, offer another simple but grand gesture that echoes the house's iron hardware.

Peri's confidence in mixing the old and the new, the bold and the precious, is what makes her style so distinctive and fresh. In the front hall, for example, a simple, modern oversize round mirror is underlined by a row of small cast-iron Boston terrier doorstops. In the bathroom, a row of hand-shaped candy dishes becomes a distinctive frieze around the long, sleek tub.

A guest cottage on the property is a romantic retreat cozily paneled in dark pine.

With simple white furnishings and its own bath and kitchenette, it is much in demand by visiting family and friends.

Besides the soft whir of ceiling fans, the chirping of crickets at night, and the glow of the fire on a rainy evening, perhaps what's most romantic about this haven is its ocean-side setting, and all the idyllic activities it engenders. Every morning, no matter what the weather, Charley and Peri take their dogs for a long walk along the beach. "There's nothing like it," says Peri, "in all different kinds of light, weather, or times of the year."

Like their work, their passion for collecting, their love of entertaining, and even their decorating, their house is a joint venture, sometimes amiably debated, but always a labor of love.

ABOVE: *On the porch, "our summer living room," a big round table covered with a white matelassé bedspread is the place to be—and eat—in the summer.*
RIGHT: *Since Peri and Charley own two Tibetan terriers, they gravitate toward dog-themed collectibles like the cast-iron Boston terrier doorstops in the hall.*
FOLLOWING PAGES: *Transferware plates and ironstone pitchers, instead of books, line the living room shelves, proving both pretty and practical for entertaining.*

Isn't It Romantic?

Displaying multiples of things to create a
feeling of generosity and abundance

A collection with personality and charm, like
the Boston terrier doorstops

The delicate patterns of transferware plates
lined along shelves like pictures

A front porch as comfortably furnished as a
living room, with gliders, wicker, and
Adirondack chairs, all with cushions and pillows

Immaculate, white, uncluttered backgrounds

The affordable extravagance of half a dozen
vases filled with brilliant sunflowers

A romantic guest-cottage aerie with spare white
furnishings, a ceiling fan, and the soft glow of
white paper lanterns

ABOVE: *Worn, weathered whites on everything from a cast-iron garden urn to a
woven picnic basket imbue a new home with old-house character.*
RIGHT: *Black base cabinets give classic white country beadboard a more sophisticated edge. The marble-topped center island/work table has graced many of Peri
and Charley's kitchens.*
FOLLOWING PAGES: *The antique folding table in the dining room might once
have been used at cricket matches or in a grange hall.*

Symmetry and repetition elevate *the ordinary:*
Sunflowers interspersed with votives
create impact *on a long table.*

A SOUND TRACK FOR SEDUCTION

Pop one of these into the CD player and you'll instantly set the right mood:

Charles Aznavour: *Toi et Moi*

Andrea Bocelli: *Romanza*

The Bodyguard sound track

Buena Vista Social Club sound track

Harry Connick Jr.: *20*

Hôtel Costes series

Enya: *Paint the Sky with Stars*

Serge Gainsbourg: *Couleur Café*

Marvin Gaye: *I Want You; Let's Get It On*

Al Green: *Greatest Hits*

Julio Iglesias: *Crazy*

Chris Isaak: *Baja Sessions*

Johnny Mathis: *16 Most Requested Songs*

Johnny Mercer: *Capitol Collectors Series*

Luis Miguel: *Vivo; Mis Romances*

Van Morrison: *Moondance*

Willie Nelson: *Stardust*

Out of Africa sound track

Elvis Presley: *The 50 Greatest Love Songs*

Rachmaninoff: *Piano Concertos Nos. 2 and 3*

Eros Ramazzotti: *Stile Libero*

Smokey Robinson: *A Quiet Storm*

Linda Ronstadt: *What's New*

Roxy Music: *Avalon*

Sade: *Lovers Rock; The Best of Sade*

Jimmy Scott: *All the Way*

Percy Sledge: *The Best of Percy Sledge*

Luther Vandross: *The Night I Fell in Love*

LEFT: *Rustic pine walls in the guest cottage form a warm backdrop for inexpensive crisp white furnishings.*

ABOVE: *Peri turned her collection of hand-shaped candy dishes, made at the turn of the century by Westmoreland Glass, into a whimsical border in the bathroom.*

Modern Romance

Here's proof that femininity, charm, and creature comforts can happily coexist with clean lines, uncluttered surfaces, and simple backgrounds, whether pure white or saturated with color. Instead of overdoing the frills and flourishes, simplify and edit for a more updated take on romance.

LEFT AND ABOVE: *First Mary Mulcahy found the perfect shade of yellow, then she adapted a chinoiserie-inspired pattern from a Swedish book and had a friend stencil it onto the walls, creating an inspired backdrop that echoes the curlicues of the dining room chandelier.*

WITH A FRENCH ACCENT

What is it about all things French that makes them so stylish and so inherently romantic? The sense of history and tradition —the way centuries-old antiques from *grandmère* mix effortlessly with things that are modern and witty? The way color and pattern are mixed with élan? The landscape, particularly in southern France, a fragrant carpet of lavender and sunflowers? Mary Mulcahy can't quite put her finger on it—she just knows she loves *la vie française,* and she has channeled it so successfully you might never know her home is in Tucson, Arizona, and not Saint-Rémy. Because the sunny, warm climate is similar to that of her beloved Provence, she has been able to create much of the same feel in her 1929 Mediterranean stucco house, a rare older home in Tucson.

Though Mary, a talented photo stylist and art director, grew up in Minnesota, she is an ardent Francophile—she visits Paris every year, pores over French magazines, and seeks out stores and merchandise with a French accent. Her mother, who was French, had an innate sense of style that she clearly passed on to her daughter. Mary's passion for fabric and her ability to hunt down incredible bargains (qualities shared by the French) give her the freedom to experiment with different looks and change her interiors the way some people change their wardrobes. "I buy

fabric instead of clothes," she confesses, and because she can have slipcovers sewn up quite inexpensively where she lives, she can truly make over a chair for the cost of a dress: Her living room sofa is covered in fabric she found for $2 a yard and had made into a slipcover for $70. Shopping is an occupational hazard for a stylist, and great finds for her home are one of the dividends. Mary is always on the prowl for bargains at Goodwill and thrift shops rather than fancy antiques stores that don't fit her budget. She has an eye for good bones, interesting lines, and whimsical details, even when they're concealed beneath unattractive finishes. Almost everything in her home has been treated to a coat of paint, a slipcover, or both. And things rarely stay the same for long. Mary's spirit of invention and willingness to experiment give her home a fresh, charming persona. What she calls "unsophisticated colors"—sunny yellows, cherry reds, and classic blues, all crisply leavened with white—become the epitome of chic in her capable hands.

In a household dominated by testosterone (she and her husband, Mike, have two sons, ages twelve and thirteen), whose decor might otherwise be dictated by ESPN, Mary has unapologetically applied feminine, romantic touches, but her use of clean, strong

Thanks to the temperate weather in Tucson, Mary can keep upholstered furniture on her covered porch, which makes it feel like another room.

colors and the absence of frills and ruffles keep the mood modern and bright. Tendrils of ivy wend their way around the living room's oversize picture window, and all of the windows and doorways are framed by interior shutters in the European fashion. Candles and chandeliers illuminate with a soft glow. In one particularly winning touch, panels of chinoiserie-inspired curlicues are stenciled in white on the dining room's sunflower walls. Richly patterned, exotic encaustic cement tiles, like the kind seen in old-fashioned French houses (and which Mary tracked down at a bargain price in Mexico), line the kitchen and bathroom floors. The sofa and bureau profiles boast feminine curves, and comfortable, come-hither pillows are everywhere. A plump, toile-covered chair even sits at the ready in the bath. And the outdoors is just as inviting: Cushy upholstered seating furnishes the terrace.

Throughout the once-dark house, Mary's primary aim has been to bring in light, openness, and cheering color, though in winter she cozies up the palette, introducing more reds and golds, touches of leopard, and patterned rugs. And here and there, the careful eye can always detect a hint of her muse, *la France,* from the black-and-white photograph of a fountain at Versailles in the entry to the portrait of a Napoleonic soldier in the kitchen. Though she'd rather be living in Paris, Mary has clearly conjured up the next best thing.

Mary mixes red, her signature shade, with lots of white and brings out its charm in gingham checks, ticking stripes, and winsome patterns like the clothesline silhouette on the throw pillow. Tall shutters and a fringe of ivy frame the view outside the large picture window.

48

DIME-STORE ROMANCE
Thrills and chills on the cheap:

Candy hearts

Faux pearls

The view of the Statue of Liberty from the
Staten Island Ferry

Picnics

Poetry

Daisies

Photo booths

Ferris wheels, roller coasters,
and merry-go-rounds

Reading aloud to each other

Back rubs and foot massages

Flirting

Boardwalks

Fireworks

Sparklers

Drive-in movies

Two straws in a milk shake

Glow-in-the-dark jewelry

Jumping the waves

Old-fashioned valentines

TOP LEFT: *Pale lavender walls, a toile quilt hung
on the wall, plantation shutters, and a curvy
little French chair hint at, rather than holler,
femininity in the bedroom.*
LEFT: *Mary created a bold patchwork in the
laundry room using encaustic tiles found in
Mexico for a fraction of the cost of French ones.*
RIGHT: *A black-and-white chinoiserie toile
chair and tin lamp bring sophisticated style to
the bath.*

Isn't It Romantic?

Lipstick red, revealing a more innocent side in gingham and paisley

Chandeliers, both electrified and with candles

Plantation shutters that offer the pleasure of closing them for privacy or opening them to the view

French Louis-anything chairs dressed down in bright, informal fabrics

Extralong, enveloping sofas

Touches of France—photographs, souvenirs, pictures, accessories

Toile

Stenciled embellishments on the walls that are sophisticated, not cutesy

Walls lined with personal mementos, especially in a personal space like an office

LEFT: *One end of the large living room serves as a work area where Mary can meet with clients. A boldly scaled trestle table is brightened with re-covered reproduction French chairs.*

TOP RIGHT: *A dressing alcove off the bedroom is Mary's personal office, where she lines the walls with photographs, her children's artwork, and other personal mementos.*

RIGHT: *Bold awning stripes and a leopard-print chair add spark to the guest room.*

SEDUCED BY THE SUN

When lifelong East Coast residents move to southern California, they are often immediately seduced by the sun—the way it shines the vast majority of the time; the warm, balmy days even in January; the giddy luxury of consigning down parkas and winter boots to long-term storage. But what they sometimes miss (besides the variety of four seasons) is the sense of history and architectural character. When Kim Fiscus and her husband, Bruce, moved from Philadelphia to Laguna Beach, they fell in love with California, but they spent three years searching for a house with enough intrinsic charm and personality to feel like "home." Kim, who owns an eponymous home furnishings store, finally found one of the original Laguna Beach cottages, and knew this two-bedroom 1936 house was it. "It just felt good," says Kim, who savors the way the sunlight pours into every room, the airy peaked ceilings that reach to the roofline, and the easy give-and-take between indoors and out.

The only constraints are those of size: The couple have carefully accounted for every inch of the less than 1,400 square feet of their home, imbuing it with a spacious, airy sensibility. Kim and Bruce even sacrificed several closets (they're down to only two) to make every room as large and open as possible. (All their off-season or infrequently used possessions are now crammed into the garage.) There is an upside to limited space: "Everything that Bruce and I have put in our house has special meaning to us," says Kim. "It's not about bows and ribbons. It's about a real sense of comfort and security that we create through the things we find, and how we use them." Her philosophy offers a definition of modern romance as real and heartfelt as any you're likely to find.

Kim solved her home's spatial challenges through a variety of strategies: In the living room, a quartet of intriguing chairs—one of her collecting passions—engage in a more lively dialogue than would a space-eating sofa. Two small glass end tables that seem to virtually float in space replace a standard coffee table. Books, another love, are neatly concentrated on one full wall of bookshelves added by Kim and Bruce. The consistent backdrop of white walls, bare wooden floors,

In the tiny bedroom, a serene white bed dressed in poppy-strewn linens seems to float on air. The headboard is actually a painting by friend Denny Ekstrom.
FOLLOWING PAGES, CLOCKWISE FROM TOP LEFT: *Bookshelves display an array of intriguing vignettes; since Kim and Bruce moved to California, palm trees have become a favorite icon. The couple treasures their highly collectible beaded sailor's valentine. Kim uses mannequins to display jewelry at the store and at home. A necklace of ivory beads ornaments an open book.*

"Most of the things I like are **old**, but have a

*clean, almost **contemporary** feel about them.”*

and uncovered windows all contribute to the feeling of openness.

Kim is a talented designer who proves the adage that you should fill a small space with a few large, statement-making pieces instead of lots of small odds and ends. For example, at the dining end of the room, a generous 9-foot table accommodates dinners for ten or big projects, but the long banquette/window seat is a great space-saver. In the diminutive master bedroom, the clean-lined white bed (there's not even room for a bureau) takes center stage, and the small size of the room creates a snug, sensuous oasis.

Part of what makes this house so romantic is the easygoing relationship it enjoys with the outdoors. The master bedroom opens onto the front garden, the guest bedroom/home office opens onto the deck, and big windows throughout the house erase much of the boundary between indoors and out. Charming, comfortable wicker chairs and a table surrounded by kumquat trees on the deck make dining en plein air an everyday luxury. Fresh flowers and topiaries bring splashes of color indoors, and even the vintage palm-tree prints and pillow fabrics offer subtle reminders of nature.

Throughout their twelve-year courtship and into their marriage, Kim and Bruce have always gone to flea markets together on weekends, and he just accompanied her for the first time on a buying trip to Europe. "Our house is truly a collaboration," says Kim. "Everything means something to us."

Kim loves chairs, and often has intriguing pieces, like this 1940s tufted leather chair, copied to sell in her store. The others are copied from an antique. Bookshelves across one wall add interest while managing collections.

DRESSED TO THRILL

Sure, stiletto heels are sexy, but sometimes so are flip-flops.

Camisoles

Slip dresses

High boots

Anything sheer

Short skirts, short shorts

Leather jacket or pants, but not head to toe

Hip-hugging pants

Cashmere sweaters

Tuxedos

Bikinis

Pareos

Backless or strapless dresses

Silk and velvet

A man's button-down shirt, unbuttoned

LEFT: *An old cherry farm table from France and turn-of-the-century French chairs that "have a contemporary feel about them" stretch the length of the bay window, where Kim added banquette seating.*

ABOVE: *Though she finds antique wicker can't withstand regular outdoor use, Kim added cushions of antique military linen to new wicker chairs on the deck. The Astier pitcher is from a French pottery like she carries in her store.*

Isn't It Romantic?

*An extra-long window-seat alcove that serves
as seating for dinner or lounging*

Old leather-bound books

*A bedroom that's almost entirely bed, with
everything in shades of white*

*One-of-a-kind pieces that are pure whimsy,
such as the homemade chandelier in the
bedroom or the beaded sailor's valentine*

*Slipcovers made from antique linens, such as
homespun French convent sheets*

*Jewelry displayed as art, not hidden away
in a drawer*

*Tropical flora such as kumquat trees,
flowering hibiscus, and palm trees*

Using your best silver every day

TOP LEFT: *In the home office/guest room, French
doors open up onto an ocean view.*
LEFT: *Kim often fashions slipcovers from antique
textiles, such as these from homespun linen
French convent sheets; the pillow is also made
from vintage fabric.*
RIGHT: *A beautifully worn butcher's block from
France, probably from the 1860s, forms the
perfect narrow island in the kitchen. Glass-
fronted corner cabinets display heirloom silver
and cookbooks.*

A PURITY
OF VISION

*M*ost people view decorating as a process of addition and acquisition, but for Los Angeles designer Karin Blake, it seems more a process of subtraction and distillation. She has been a collector of fine early-American folk art and furniture for much of her adult life, and her spare, carefully edited home in Malibu serves as a gallery-like backdrop for her best and favorite pieces.

While others would look at a Spanish-style house simply for what it was, Karin saw how she could remake this one to suit her own vision of modern simplicity. She gave curved walls and arched doorways crisp right angles; replaced all the windows with clean-lined commercial steel casements that welcome in even more light; and laid sleek, gray-slate floors throughout the first floor, which she says are ideal for both the beach and pets. "I completely gutted the kitchen and put in a wall of windows and a huge skylight. I can't get enough light," she avows. "There's nothing worse than being in a dark kitchen in the morning." She installed a glass-block shower in the downstairs bath so even that room is filled with light.

New commercial steel windows and a skylight flood the kitchen with sunshine. The contrast between old and new is what makes this home so intriguing: Old glove molds line up beneath the range hood; a carved horse graces the island.

The streamlined and simplified architectural shell provides a pure white foil for the weathered paint, timeworn edges, and whimsical charm of her folk art and furniture collections. While the stark contrast of old and new may seem unexpected, the rocking horses, whirligigs, and old shooting-gallery targets bring warmth and humanity to the monastic simplicity of the architecture, while the clean, white, uncluttered canvas provides the light and space in which to truly appreciate Karin's remarkable pieces. The fireplace is a perfect case in point: Karin replaced its cold marble surround with a painted antique mantel, moving the top of the mantel beneath the firebox to frame the eye-level hearth.

Part of Karin's motivation in keeping things simple was to make maintenance easier, because she and her husband also own a ranch in Montana. "Since we travel a lot, I wanted a turnkey home," says Karin. In fact, her home base is Malibu, and her husband's is Montana. They each visit the other at least one weekend a month, and family holidays are divvied up between the two homes as well. As other cou-ples have often discovered, their absences keep the romance alive.

Of course, in Malibu, romance is inherent in the beach and the ocean, which is just across the street from the Blakes' home. They also have a pool, purposely kept spare and simple for the same ease of upkeep. "I like Malibu because it's a small town next to a big city," says Karin. "I like the community feeling, the fact that you can bike everywhere." And being on the ocean makes "being at home like a vacation."

But for Karin, passion also comes from the pleasure of being surrounded by folk art and furnishings, carefully collected over a lifetime, that embody the history of other people and places. "It's like being in my own private gallery, and it gives me incredible pleasure. I love the paint and colors of folk art, the fact that it's handmade and one-of-a-kind. It's what I grew up with as a child in Bucks Country, Pennsylvania, and it has just always stayed with me. There is a whimsy and sense of humor in a lot of folk art that makes you smile—it's not so serious."

LEFT: *Karin reinvented a modern marble fireplace with an antique red-painted mantel. The fireplace can be seen from the kitchen as well.*
ABOVE: *A collection of firkins steps up the stairs to the master bedroom; the landing is crowned with an old game board.*

Isn't It Romantic?

*Collections carefully acquired over decades,
where each piece has personal meaning*

*Large, tilt-in casement windows that fill each
room with greenery and abundant light*

*Clean, uncluttered rooms that create
low-maintenance style*

*Folk art that reveals a sense of whimsy and
unschooled charm*

A deep clawfoot tub

*A clean-lined, uncovered tester bed—a modern
take on the old-fashioned canopy—with
crisp white linens*

An eye-level fireplace in the dining room

*Primitive folk-art toys that connect
us to our childhood*

*Living in a beach community
year-round*

*Karin added a new living room to balance the
house plan; it faces the mountains to the north.
An antique architectural vent and its twin copy
create what Karin calls "instant decorating"
on a long wall.*

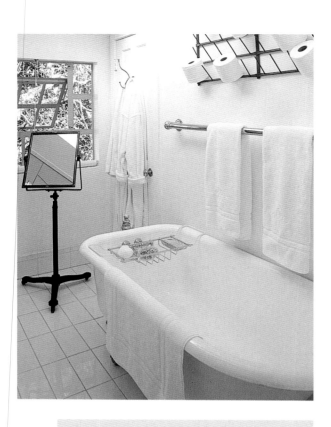

CLASSIC COUPLES

Like peanut butter and jelly or gin and tonic,
these twosomes are so memorable we often
think of them in tandem:

Lucy & Ricky   Barbie & Ken
Hepburn & Tracy   Burns & Allen
Roy & Dale   Fred & Wilma
Fred & Ginger   Ozzie & Harriet
Bogart & Bacall   Newman &
Romeo & Juliet   Woodward
Sonny & Cher   Adam & Eve

ABOVE: *What was once a meat rack now holds*
extra rolls of toilet paper in the bath.
RIGHT: *Karin copied the bed after an antique,*
making it more architectural. Some of her
favorite pieces reside in her bedroom, including a
model of an old livery stable (bottom shelf),
probably made for a child, and a whirligig with
riders on horseback (on the bedside table).

THE ARTIST'S HAND

On a bustling street near the University of Arizona campus in Tucson, if you look closely, you may see a lush bower of the palest yellow Tombstone roses almost obscuring a set of terra-cotta steps. Duck under the fragrant, verdant arch, open the iron gate, brush past the palms, and you have arrived at a 1935 Spanish-style bungalow that seems more like a vacation hideaway than the home of an active family of four. Thanks to artist and photo stylist Paula Hamilton's globetrotting imagination and deft touch with a paintbrush and sewing machine, this house exudes a Mediterranean air of exotic romance.

Paula and her husband, Gordon, have added to their bungalow over time, converting the garage into Paula's art studio, then adding a family room that connects the house to the garage, creating a U-shaped courtyard. One of their most brilliant decisions was to turn a tiny, sun-parched yard into a cooling oasis with a pool and terrace and an ingenious improvised cabana that makes guests feel as though they've suddenly been transported to the Greek isles. Paula built the cabana herself for about $500 by simply lashing a roof of bamboo fencing onto posts and adding a fringe of dried palm fronds.

Inside the house, Paula has whitewashed nearly everything for the same airy island appeal, though bits of pure, saturated color here and there, like the brilliant fuchsia in the kitchen, add a sexy jolt of energy.

Intriguing architectural details, such as the varied and unusual doors, the book-lined niches (some of them filled-in windows), and the beamed ceilings, contribute to the house's intrinsic character, which is underscored by the eclectic mix of furniture, much of it found at tag sales, inherited, or reinvented in some way by Paula. She slipcovered all the living room furniture with an entire bolt of ticking fabric found at a bargain outlet; the coffee table was uncovered in a garage, and the bench was bought generations ago by Gordon's family in Mexico.

Faced with any necessity, Paula responds with resourceful invention: When she couldn't find a tablecloth long enough for the dining table, she made her own from a French *boutis* (quilt). Inexpensive straw rugs become something special with a simple painted border; motifs painted freehand on the kitchen walls give them the spice of an Indian sari. Chandeliers (with candles in the dining room), ceiling fans (instead of central air), and French doors leading from nearly every ground-floor room to the pool and welcom-

Beneath the poolside cabana, a farmhouse table with rush-seated chairs invites shaded meals and drinks alfresco. Paula covered banquettes and chaises in a refreshing blue-and-white stripe, stitched a blue border onto a basic white tablecloth, and painted a blue outline onto inexpensive straw rugs.

ing the oleander-scented breeze, all imbue the house with romance, while the bare floors and simple white curtains don't interrupt the mood.

The sun-drenched, outdoor-centered life in Arizona has much in common with that of the Mediterranean, so the Hamilton house seems right at home here. And yet it also gives the wonderful sense of an exotic getaway—and what could be more romantic than that?

ABOVE: *Lacy white motifs stenciled on the windows (with washable latex paint), a common touch in Mexico and the Southwest, add feminine charm as well as privacy.*
RIGHT: *Bamboo fencing, dried palm fronds, and curtains of white muslin create an exotic cabana (and respite from the sun) for less than $500.*

Isn't It Romantic?

A tile-lined turquoise pool

An open-air, curtained cabana by the pool

*French doors connecting each room
to the courtyard*

*Walls painted in seductive shades like
fuchsia and patterned with freehand motifs*

Lush plantings of roses, oleander, and palms

*Table lamps and candles in the kitchen and
dining room instead of overhead lighting*

*Ceiling fans and windows open to the breeze
instead of air-conditioning*

*Painted white "lace" on windows
for pretty privacy*

*Snuggling a bed into an alcove, even
in a large bedroom*

*An outdoor "room" furnished with a long,
pillow-strewn banquette for lounging*

*Channeling the Greek Isles or another
exotic spot in your home*

*A friend found an entire bolt of ticking fabric
at a bargain outlet and sent it to Paula, who
gave her living room uniformity by using it to
slipcover every piece of furniture.*

THE MOST ROMANTIC GETAWAYS STATESIDE

When you want to get away from it all and recharge your romance, here's where to indulge:

Arizona Inn, Tucson, Arizona

L'Auberge de Sedona, Sedona, Arizona

Royal Palms, Phoenix, Arizona

Auberge du Soleil, Napa Valley, California

Hotel Bel-Air, Los Angeles

Korakia Pensione, Palm Springs, California

Manka's, Inverness, California

Shutters on the Beach, Santa Monica

Ventana Inn, Big Sur, California

Little Palm Island, Florida

Lodge at Little St. Simons Island, Georgia

Kona Village Resort, Hawaii

Hôtel Maison de Ville, New Orleans

Maison Orléans, New Orleans

Wheatleigh, Lenox, Massachusetts

The Point, Saranac Lake, New York

Sundance Resort, Sundance, Utah

Twin Farms, Barnard, Vermont

Inn at Little Washington, Washington, Virginia

Canoe Bay, Chetek, Wisconsin

Amangani, Jackson, Wyoming

LEFT: *The dining room was created by building in a covered porch. Paula fashioned the tablecloth from a French quilt, giving it a bias-tape scalloped edge. A candlelit chandelier offers seductive mood lighting.*

ABOVE: *Wine bottles mingle with votive candles on a tray for entertaining. Paula painted motifs on the pink walls of the kitchen to create the look of wallpaper.*

FOLLOWING PAGES, LEFT: *"Everything was wood or beige when we moved in," says Paula. "I just painted it all white." In the long master bedroom, she nestled the bed inside an alcove for coziness; books fill former window niches.*

RIGHT: *Studies of coffee cups and other paintings by Paula are tacked up in her studio.*

A MARRIAGE OF STYLES

$\mathcal{I}$n many marriages, one spouse is more interested than the other in the design and decoration of the house (often, though certainly not always, the woman). In other marriages, the process is a collaboration, which works well when both partners share similar tastes, but is much more of a challenge when they don't. In the case of Jean and Patton Brooks, their collaboration is a natural one. Pat is a residential architect who has redone much of their house wielding little more than a Craftsman drill, and Jean has a passion for decorating and gardening in her spare time. Together, they have remade their small 1940s Houston bungalow into a serene, inviting home.

"In 1969, when we first married and moved in, we figured we wouldn't be here for that long," remembers Jean. "But we wound up loving our neighborhood and never leaving." Over the years, Pat has enhanced their small, 1,700-square-foot home with numerous renovations. He converted the garage into a high-ceilinged room that now serves as one of two living areas. He installed windows, whitewashed the ceiling, added beams, and put a carport in front to replace the garage. In the other cozy living room/den in the back of the house, he put in a fireplace, opened up the space to the kitchen, took out the knotty pine walls, and put in

larger windows recycled from an old building. After recent flood damage, he whitewashed their floors, which lightened things up even further.

Meanwhile, Jean worked her magic on the back terrace. Defying Houston's sometimes oppressive heat, she turned it into a cooling green oasis with a European sensibility. There is a lush rose garden, along with an abundance of carefully pruned boxwood, topiaries, ivy, and jasmine. "Pat draws up the design, and I do the installation," says Jean, who was particularly proud when a French visitor pronounced her garden *"très Français."*

Pat and Jean have also collaborated on furniture, such as the tray tables in the living room and bath, which Pat designed and built and Jean faux-painted. The process hasn't always been completely smooth sailing, however: When they were first married, Pat had more contemporary furniture and Jean was partial to French antiques and traditional design. "I waited him out," admits Jean, a strategy she still uses today. For example, Pat wasn't sure about the dramatically scaled mirror, originally from a French château, in their living room. Jean's strategy: Put it in place, and eventually Pat will get used to it.

Though Jean once had a lot more "stuff" in the house, including a lot of pictures on the walls, she says, "I really like hav-

In a garage converted into an elegant, high-ceilinged living room, a mirror from a French château makes a dramatic, light-reflecting focal point.

Isn't It Romantic?

One dramatic gesture, such as the nearly floor-to-ceiling, elaborately carved antique French mirror in the living room

Lots of table lamps, even in the kitchen

A secluded terrace planted with a topiary garden and romantic roses for cutting

In the bath, tray tables and étagères filled with wicker baskets and silver-topped jars

Tall windows and French doors that provide views of the garden

A quiet, serene, creamy palette

LEFT: *All-white linens in the bedroom create an ethereal retreat, with a simple mirror serving as a headboard. French doors open up to the garden.* ABOVE: *White epoxy paint inexpensively camouflaged unattractive pink tile in the bath.*

ing things clean now—very simple and tai-lored. I use everything—nothing is just for show." Her style has evolved from patterned fabrics and lots of accessories to become more monochromatic and spare. "It's so hot here; this palette is very cooling and peaceful," she points out, and, like the sea-grass carpeting throughout most of the house, it gives a small home a sense of continuity and openness.

Jean is a master of reinvention: She inexpensively redid the bathroom's "shocking pink" tile by painting over it with white epoxy. She has had her original Wicker Works sofa and ottoman for years and has redone the cushions five or six times— they're now a natural linen. And she trans-formed the formerly brown-and-white-check bedroom into an all-white haven.

Jean has made the most of the house's compact space through the generous use of mirrors. In addition to the dramatic room-defining mirror in the living room, she has had several mirrors made with simple frames in custom sizes: One serves as a headboard above their bed; another is placed above the fireplace in the den; and a tall, narrow mirror brightens the bathroom. In every room, mir-rors reflect light and expand the space.

The end result is a home that feels pulled together but not "done." "I don't like things that feel too decorator-y," says Jean. In fact, it's the small touches, such as the olive tree topiaries grown by Jean and used as table decorations at their son's wedding, or the tables she and Pat have crafted together, that make the Brookses' home a true labor of love.

LEFT: *A tailored celadon-and-cream stripe provides just a soft hint of color in the den, where woven baskets and a sea-grass rug add texture.*
ABOVE: *Lamp light sets copper pots aglow in the kitchen.*

Screen Gems

Romantic Classics

They just don't make 'em like they used to:

An Affair to Remember
The African Queen
Breakfast at Tiffany's
Brief Encounter
Casablanca
Doctor Zhivago
Gone With the Wind
Jules and Jim
Love Story
A Man and a Woman
Now, Voyager
Roman Holiday
Sayonara
Summer of '42
Wuthering Heights

Chick Flicks

These romantic films are good enough to
entertain both of you:

Body Heat
Dirty Dancing
The English Patient
The French Lieutenant's Woman
The Goodbye Girl
An Officer and a Gentleman
Out of Africa
The Piano
Sense and Sensibility
Sleepless in Seattle
The Way We Were
The Year of Living Dangerously

*Jean adapted these charming heart-backed
student chairs by replacing their leather seats
with pierced iron for outdoor use.*

Old-World Romance

Travel across continents and centuries brings the romance of the past into homes of today—offering the pleasure of collecting and living with objects that have witnessed other eras and cultures, enriching our own. Skillful collectors weave objects from many different places and periods into an intricate, memorable, one-of-a-kind tapestry.

ABOVE: *In Kay O'Toole's home, symmetry creates a pleasing composition of eighteenth-century Italian chairs, mirror, and sconces.*
RIGHT: *French Madonna crowns etch lacy silhouettes on a 1940s French lattice garden table that Kay stripped to its pewtery base.*

NESTING INSTINCTS

For those who despair of creating a romantic atmosphere because they live in a post-war apartment, take heart. Step into Kay O'Toole's home in Houston, and you could well think you are in an old Paris town house in the venerable *quartier* of Le Marais. Like an old master's drawing, her home is sketched in chiaroscuro and grisaille, a subtle play of light and shadow wrought in infinite shades of gray. While some might consider gray somber, Kay finds it "very restful and serene." The furnishings are fine French and Italian antiques, thanks to Kay's profession as an antiques dealer, yet they are covered predominantly in a simple quilted dove-gray cotton. This not only makes them approachable and practical for everyday use but also serves to unite disparate pieces and styles and showcase the beauty of each piece's worn finish and elegant lines. The curtains, however, are the most luxurious pale gray silk, cascading onto the floor like ball gowns. As in her shop, Kay O'Toole Antiques and Eccentricities, every corner of her apartment cradles handfuls of intriguing riches, and each piece has its own story to tell.

When Kay moved into this apartment in a 1950s building seven years ago, it didn't have much architectural detail, though it did have good light and an enchanting view of a huge magnolia tree outside its generous windows. She set about bestowing upon it her European sensibility, and then a year ago, she was able to purchase the apartment across the hall and break through to create a single spacious residence. Her living room is now doubled in size, with outdoor balconies at either end, and a partial wall in the middle that she has mirrored on both sides to reflect light into the apartment. Like a grand salon, the living room is informally divided into a variety of distinct seating areas: from a Napoleon III settee paired with eighteenth-century bergères, to a long, languorous early-nineteenth-century French daybed with peeling paint, to chairs loosely gathered around a table covered with an Aubusson rug.

Kay added all the architectural details the space lacked. Windows are framed in old French shutters that stretch from floor to ceiling, which, she says, "helped more than anything else we did to make it feel less apartment-like." She outlined the plain doors throughout the apartment as well as her bedroom walls in picture-frame molding to imbue them with more character, and six

RIGHT: *Kay's eye for intrigue is evident in the cast-iron shell filled with fossilized ferns, tin palm fronds peering out from a zinc urn, and the table covered in an Aubusson rug, which Kay says hides all manner of spills.*

FOLLOWING PAGES: *Quilted dove-gray cotton unifies a Napoleon III settee and eighteenth-century walnut bergères; taupe Fortuny damask covers the side chair.*

ornate yellow-and-gray columns made of papier-mâché that were once used as stage decoration also help define the space. She gravitates toward unusual architectural ornaments that layer three-dimensional richness into the rooms, such as stone pedestals and column bases supporting statues and planters. Bare parquet floors throughout the apartment suit Houston's hot climate, as well as her dog. A faux-finish painter stained a dark grid on the floors to give them more impact. "The rooms look bigger without rugs because there's the same flooring throughout," Kay points out.

Though nearly every piece in her home has a distinguished pedigree, "It's always been the more informal things that I've liked," says Kay. "Not bronze ormolu, but painted provincial furniture that you can see

is handmade. Each piece has its own story: You can see where the wood is darker or lighter where it was used, or how the top has been patched, or the legs worn down. You can see the evidence of the tools used to carve it." She confidently mixes twentieth-century garden tables and 1930s lamps festooned with china roses with Louis XVI settees and eighteenth-century bergères as well as works by modern artists. "It all shares the same mood—a little worn, romantic, European. They are things that create a feeling of tranquillity. In my shop as well, I like to sell things that have a personality, so that a piece makes a difference when it goes home —it doesn't get lost."

Kay has a passion for old Fortuny fabrics and for birds. She is always on the prowl for the gracefully worn, "no color" Fortuny

ABOVE, FROM LEFT: *The woman in blue is from Mexico, probably nineteenth century. Painted Mexican angel wings float above an Italian wrought-iron table in the entry. One of Kay's many birds, this one by artist Gary Rethero.*
RIGHT: *The dining chairs are covered in cotton Fortuny damask, as is the table. Artist Lisa Ludwig made the wedding cake decorated with safety matches.*
FOLLOWING PAGES: *Kay added the molding in the master bedroom, and had curtains, a bedspread, and a headboard made from a bolt of old Fortuny fabric.*

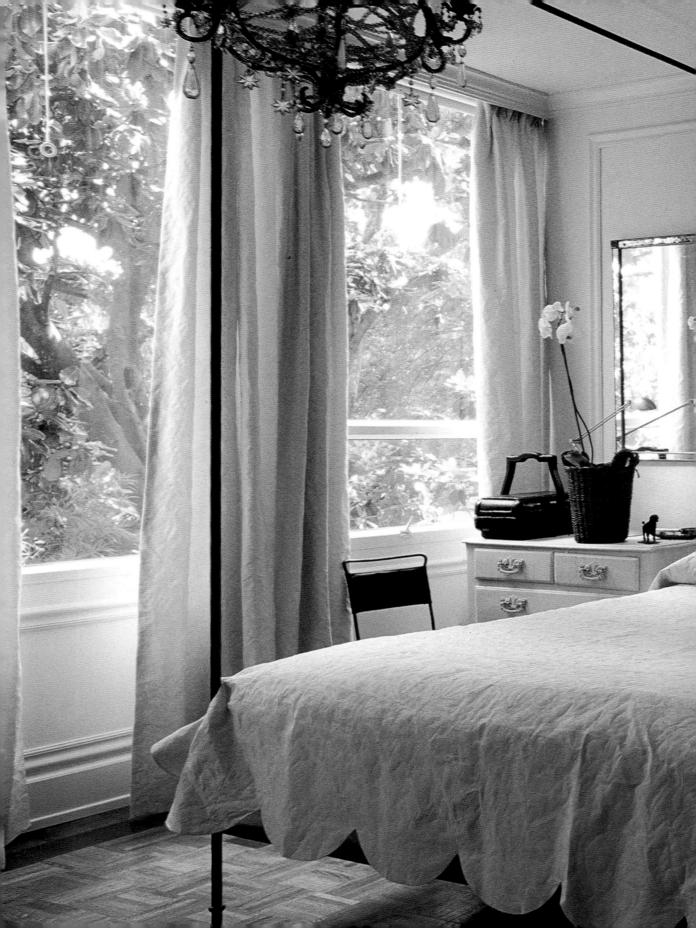

FABRICS THAT BEG TO BE TOUCHED

Sensual fabrics add tactile appeal to a romantic room:

Silk	Embroidered fabrics
Satin	Trims: fringe, beading, crochet
Linen	Leopard print
Cashmere, pashmina, angora	Toile
Fur (faux or real)	Paisley
Suede	Vintage floral barkcloth
Lace	Organza
Leather	Taffeta
Sheer fabrics	Velvet

damasks, seen on her dining room curtains, tablecloth, and chairs, though they are becoming harder to find. Her biggest thrill was discovering a whole bolt of Fortuny that allowed her to cover everything in her bedroom in the same fabric.

The birds arrive in a more serendipitous fashion, often as gifts, and her collection extends from stone, plaster, and wooden birds to found birds' nests and an incredible naturalist's case filled with eggs. "I like birds because they have nests," Kay theorizes. "One of the things that attracted me to this apartment was the magnolia tree outside, with all kinds of birds building nests in it. Birds are always adding to their nests. As an antiques dealer, I wish people did that, too!"

As lush and layered as Kay's artful vignettes are, she is a careful editor as well. Her bedroom is simple and spare: An airy iron canopy bed dominates the space, giving it a quiet grandeur. Her palette of grays with a few judicious touches of color is a testament to her rigorous eye.

Kay's definition of the moody, evocative romance that suffuses her home is beautifully poetic: "Part of it is the aged finishes, which make the rooms seem timeless. Part of it is the subtle color that makes it feel like a memory or a dream. Part of it is the comfort—that everything feels good, and there are lots of places where you can sit and read or write a letter, and have a place to put down your cup. And finally, there are so many things that refer to places I've visited or to friends that resonate with wonderful memories." Like Paris, with its meandering streets and buildings steeped in the stories of so many lives, Kay O'Toole's home has the feeling of a wonderful journey you never want to end.

China rose lamps from the 1930s are "a little over-the-top," admits Kay, who has a collection of French faience flowers such as these. The peaches and flowers in the bronze tray are china as well.

Isn't It Romantic?

Elegant French antiques given modern clarity with a subtle quilted gray cotton

Luxurious silk curtains that puddle extravagantly on the floor

Stacks of eighteenth-century hand-cut books

A charming personal signature, like the birds and nests Kay collects

Pieces that have earned their genuine, centuries-old patina

Venetian mirrors with ornately etched glass; mirrors with old silvered glass

The understated elegance of pale Fortuny damasks

Worn, silvery metals—in everything from old garden tables to palm fronds

A simple iron canopy bed that nearly grazes the ceiling paired with the comfort of a curvy upholstered headboard

Collections, like an interesting conversation, that leave you wanting to know more

FAR LEFT: *Kay created the table by adding an octagonal wooden top to a stone column and base. A naturalist's case filled with birds' eggs rests atop it.*
LEFT: *Mixing it up: A modern painting, the bust of a French general, and a cast-iron shell sink basin crown a pair of French corner cabinets.*

AN INVENTIVE SPIRIT

*D*onna Temple Brown, a Houston antiques dealer, had always lived in old homes. But her work has taught her to be open to new ideas: "Otherwise the search is more difficult and you waste a lot of time looking for something you might not find," she says. When Donna began looking for homes in the community she loved near her store, The Gray Door, she found that all the old houses were not only very expensive but also in need of extensive renovation. So she broadened her search and ended up buying a new town house that offered 10-foot-high ceilings, generous space, and architectural details such as French doors and moldings. Then she ripped out almost everything else, including items that would be selling points for most people—built-in bookcases in the living room, built-in cabinets in the powder room, and the entire kitchen, including all the cabinets, the pantry, and the angled walls that were designed to "liven up" the space. In place of all the developer built-ins, she used antique furnishings to create a richer and more personal setting.

Many of the pieces Donna commandeered for her new house were "orphans" from her shop that no one else could figure out how to use. In the big, open, inviting kitchen, a French *comptoir* (shop counter) became an island and now holds the sink and dishwasher, with shelves installed in back for storage. A French wine rack became open shelving for tableware with the substitution of metal shelves for some of the bottle racks. A 10-foot-long English baker's counter whose size intimidated clients now runs from the kitchen into the seating area, bringing continuity to the space as well as extensive storage. Nothing is standard, ready-made, or new: Small iron grates hold spice bottles on the walls. A large French armoire hides a small TV, table linens, and baskets of candles. An antique pot rack from a Midwest butcher's shop is hung like art on the wall. Donna turned the coat closet into a pantry and just uses an iron coatrack near the front door, since coats are seldom needed in Houston anyway.

Donna was looking for painted antique bookshelves to replace the modern built-ins she had removed in the living room, but always being open to serendipity, she came across tall, weathered shutters instead, which add wonderful texture and architectural drama to the room. She is having them built in as doors to conceal cabinetry for her stereo on one side of the fireplace and a bar

LEFT: *An antique American table next to the stove is lined with crocks full of utensils and trays of oils; pots and pans are stored below.*
FOLLOWING PAGES: *Instead of built-in cabinets, Donna outfitted her kitchen with unusual antiques like the French wire wine rack and a worn* comptoir.

on the other. Donna changed the polished blond wood floors to a medium-dark stain with a wax instead of a urethane finish. "I love the patina of a waxed floor," she says. "I don't mind scratches here and there. I want it to look like people live here."

Though Donna lives on her own (she's divorced with grown children), she entertains frequently and came up with a flexible seating arrangement that allows her to sit eight or more in a relatively small space. Instead of the standard couch and two club chairs, she uses a tailored love seat she's had for years and four Louis XVI carved chairs with worn gilding, upholstered in cream linen, that have a clean, modern elegance. Two nineteenth-century French garden chairs, showcased almost as sculptures against the wooden shutters, and assorted ottomans offer additional pull-up seating.

The same inventive spirit reigns in the diminutive dining room, where Donna paired a modern polished-steel table with an eighteenth-century French painted walnut bench and two Swedish chairs. The Italian chandelier, made from silver-leafed wood and iron with pendant rock crystals, was a piece from The Gray Door that she had always coveted: "I love the mood that it sets. It reminds me of a summer shower." The eighteenth-century French tapestry, on the other hand, is something she never imagined wanting, but she fell in love with it at a neighboring dealer's and it happened to fit

LEFT: *Grand gestures: A wall-size antique French tapestry creates a dramatic backdrop for dining.*
ABOVE RIGHT: *A display of Chinese polychrome celadon platters and plates that Donna has collected for years stretches to the ceiling for impact in the entry.*

CHEERS!
The sexiest drinks:

Martinis
Mojitos
Cosmopolitans
Champagne
Bellinis (in bed)
Margaritas
Campari on ice
Michelada (a Corona beer with fresh lime juice and salt around the rim)

Isn't It Romantic?

*A big, open kitchen filled with beautiful
antiques instead of cookie-cutter cabinets*

Sculptural garden furniture used indoors

An old-world tapestry hung floor to ceiling

*The weathered patina of old shutters, rusting
iron furniture, and centuries-old woods*

*An all-white living room that's anchored by
the shapely silhouettes of four antique chairs*

*Dramatic gestures, such as a floor-to-ceiling
display of Chinese porcelain*

A chandelier of delicate crystal beads

the space perfectly. Like the shutters in the living room, it adds big-scale drama. "In a small space, you can introduce bolder scale through accent pieces," suggests Donna, "such as a bench, side table, lamp, or artwork." In her own home, she created a dramatic sense of entry in a very small space by placing a slender glass-top console table against the wall and hanging a beautiful collection of Chinese polychrome celadon plates and platters in a column above it that reaches to the ceiling. "I usually like simpler things, but I've been collecting this porcelain since I was seventeen," says Donna. "I just have a passion for it."

Though French doors connect the living room to a courtyard and the kitchen and dining room to small patios, the house looks largely inward, which makes it feel cozy and nurturing. "It's a soothing atmosphere," Donna says. "I have a sense of privacy, but with the open stairwell and room plan, it all feels very connected." And even though Donna has fine antiques and beautiful collections, she doesn't want her house to feel too precious. When her son and daughter and grandchildren visit, she creates impromptu slipcovers with big drop cloths from Home Depot, so the kids feel welcome to climb on the sofas. "I want things to be used and lived with every day," says Donna. "If you love something, make it a part of your life. What are you waiting for? I don't want things that are just for company. I'm company!"

LEFT: *The swirl of an antique French garden chair stands out against weathered shutters.*
RIGHT, TOP AND BOTTOM: *Donna has always liked this tailored love seat because its silhouette looks good from all sides. Four 1840s French carved and gilded chairs provide a livelier dialogue than the standard sofa and club chairs.*

THE LAST ROMANTICS

*A*fter sixteen years of marriage, Carol and Mark Glasser are still romantics at heart: Mark sends Carol roses every week, not just on special occasions. Carol lights candles everywhere, even when company's not coming. Their home, with its flower-strewn bedroom, sensual red dining room/library, welcoming south-of-France kitchen, and soft apricot, antiques-filled living room, is the epitome of romantic decorating.

In their 1930s Georgian home in Houston, where the Glassers have lived since they were married, the overall style is cohesive, but part of the charm is that each room also has its own distinct character. Carol, an interior designer, turned her dining room into a library by lining the walls with bookshelves and painting everything a rich red. It makes for a warm and intimate dining space, especially with its view of the fire lit in the living room on cool nights.

In the living room, the peaches-and-cream tone of the walls, created with integral pigment in the plaster, comes alive in the soft glow of candle- and lamplight at night. One of Carol's favorite romantic elements, evident here, is mirrors. "Early on, when I couldn't afford the art I wanted, I collected antique mirrors," she says. "I still collect them because I love the way they reflect light." Carol prefers the old silvered glass, even (or especially) if it is quite worn, and if a new mirror has been inserted, she will replace it with an old one or one of the increasingly good reproductions available today.

The sunroom offers a completely different feeling, wrapped in windows and French doors on three sides and furnished with casual wicker furniture and sea-grass matting. Whereas the dining and living rooms come into their own at night, this is a morning room, where Carol loves to enjoy her first cup of coffee and the warmth of the early sun. "Romance isn't always winter by the fire," she points out.

Everyone really lives in the kitchen, of course, and Carol acknowledged that reality by adding a seating area and making it as inviting as a vacation in Provence. This room serves as a constantly changing canvas for

RIGHT: *The faded tones of the Oushak rug in the living room are echoed in the fabrics and the soft, warm apricot mixed into the plaster walls. Carol bought the eighteenth-century Dutch leather screen decades ago in London and still loves it.*
FOLLOWING PAGES, CLOCKWISE FROM TOP LEFT: *Ornate silver hearts and religious icons. The living room's French doors open onto the terrace. Santos, candles, and roses create a warm welcome in the entry. Carol's massive Welsh dresser has always served as a barometer of her current collecting interests.*

*"It's important to address **all** the senses: Dim the*

lights and add scented candles and great music."

Carol's passions and experiments with color and pattern. The massive Welsh dresser that lines one wall of the great room has held blue-and-white Staffordshire pottery, then white creamware and ironstone, then French faience and some delft. As the dresser goes, so goes the room, so blue-and-white fabrics have given way to brick-red cushions on water hyacinth furniture more in keeping with the ocher pots now lining the shelves. A beautiful fireplace, a TV, and more bookshelves and French doors make this the room where everyone wants to be.

On another side of the kitchen is a dining area invitingly furnished with a long window seat (a great solution for a narrow space), plumped with a lush lineup of pillows. "We live in this room," says Carol. "When it's just the two of us, we often sit by the fire and eat our dinner from tray tables. Even when we're entertaining more formally, I will often seat people at the table in the kitchen because I can dress it up with fancy china and silver, and it's cozy and inviting."

But perhaps the most romantic room in Mark and Carol's house is the master bedroom, part of the addition they did fifteen years ago, which incorporated the wonderful luxury of a fireplace. Carol lavished every surface—headboard, bed coverings, Roman shades, chairs—with a lush but muted Bennison floral that she hasn't tired of even a decade and a half later. "It's the ultimate romance to spend an entire Sunday in the bedroom reading by the fire, especially on a rainy day," says Carol.

Another item on Carol's must-have list for romance is candles. "To me, candlelight is the secret of romance," she confides. "I'd always loved candles, but it wasn't until I visited a friend's inn in Antigua, Guatemala, that I really understood the power of using them en masse. At this inn, when you arrive at night, nothing is electrified; everything is lit by candles—the steps, the hallways, the bedrooms. It's so simple, and it instantly sets

ABOVE: *An elaborately carved antique mirror in the living room is one of many.*
RIGHT: *Framed French herbiers (pressed herbs) flank the gracefully arched windows in the kitchen's dining alcove, where checks mix happily with toile.*
FOLLOWING PAGES: *Carol added louvered shutters in the dining room/library "because I wanted the red to keep going." Cushioned wicker chairs add comfort.*

a romantic tone. Even if I'm just having a few people over for dinner, I'll put candles coming up the front steps." She also likes to put out a big bowl of oranges or tangerines on her kitchen counter, as much for their fragrance as for eating—not to mention the fact that they go so well with her color scheme. "Fruit is much less expensive than flowers. Fill a bowl with citrus fruit and it will last for weeks."

Ultimately, Carol's approach to making a home romantic is two parts decorating, one part psychology: "You *can* create romance," she assures. "Communication is at the heart of romance. If you create the right atmosphere for you and your husband, one that's free of clutter, where you can sit comfortably and enjoy a glass of wine and talk at the end of the day, *that's* romantic." As she points out, "When you can create that kind of warmth, everyone wants to stay a little longer. That's what home is all about."

Airy elements like an eighteenth-century iron pastry table, metal garden tables, and even a birdcage make the sunroom feel light and open.

Isn't It Romantic?

*Candles everywhere, especially when you're
entertaining, but also just for you*

*Warm colors—terra-cotta reds, soft apricots,
golden Tuscan yellows—that flatter rooms
and skin tones, especially at night*

*Using the same wonderful fabric on every
soft surface—particularly in a bedroom*

*Fireplaces in every room where you spend
a lot of time*

*Big bowls of fruit for color, taste, and
fragrance*

*Mirrors, mirrors on the wall—to reflect
light and add architectural interest for less
than the cost of a painting*

*Topiaries—a more sophisticated alternative
to houseplants*

*One large cupboard, filled to the brim with
a favorite collection*

*A dining room turned library to spark
great conversation*

*One print—a classic Bennison floral—used on
every surface creates its own kind of elegant seren-
ity in the bedroom. A gas fireplace (because few
people want to lug logs upstairs) is a treasured
indulgence Carol added when she and Mark were
renovating. In Carol's European-influenced style,
surfaces are carefully arranged, never cluttered.*

SENTIMENTAL JOURNEY

*W*ithin the hugeness of Santa Fe, there is the smallness of Tesuque," says the woman who owns this incredible 30-acre property. "And within Tesuque is the even more rarefied landscape of the properties along the acequia." The acequia is a system of water ditches built by the Spanish in the seventeenth century to control, distribute, and share water with the Indians. Still in operation today, it carries rainwater and snow runoff from the Sangre de Cristo Mountains to the Tesuque Pueblo, creating a fertile valley that is a dramatic anomaly in this arid desert climate. "This area is removed from the day-to-day reality of its surroundings. To me, that defines romance," she says. It was the ability to have trees, green grass, lush gardens, and a farm in the middle of New Mexico that seduced her when she visited a friend living next door to where she lives now.

The original house was built in 1925 by a local artist named Theodore Van Solen. It was made of structural clay tile (once called pen tile because it was made in penitentiaries) rather than adobe. In the latter part of the nineteenth century, as the railroad reached Santa Fe, new building materials were brought from the east, and many adobe houses were capped in brick trim to give

English-style perennial gardens are able to flourish in arid Tesuque, thanks to the generous water supply of the acequia.

them a more formal look in keeping with the new plate-glass windows and fancy millwork being introduced. This style became known as Territorial, and when Houston architect Bill Anderson drew up the plans to add on to this house, he kept the renovations in harmony with this distinctive style.

Though the homeowner had grown up in the East surrounded by fine English antiques and this was a Southwestern-style house, she decided she wanted to capture the look and feel of the beautiful places she had visited in Tuscany and Provence. The styles were not incompatible: The aged stucco walls of Europe are akin to adobe, as are the wood-beamed ceilings, stone floors, and often large-scale, carved wood antique furnishings.

Once owned by songwriter Roger Miller, the house was in poor condition and an unfortunate addition across its south side in the 1970s had blocked the dramatic views of the Santa Fe ski basin and Sangre de Cristo

mountains. The new owner didn't want to destroy its history, so she stripped it down to its structural essence and started over. What had been the artist's studio, with high ceilings and good light, became a great room. She moved the fireplace, flanked it with tall, stately casement windows, and added an antique mantel found on her travels in Europe. A beautiful, old-world kitchen with limestone counters and floors and a dramatic copper range hood is situated at the opposite end of the room. A second-story master bedroom suite was added on to the one-story house to capture west-facing views all the way to Los Alamos and Colorado.

Throughout the long and painstaking renovation process, the homeowner stayed focused on her intention to re-create the aged grandeur that she had always loved in Europe; for example, she imported nineteenth-century stone floors from France. "Some have paint, some are chipped—the

ABOVE, FROM LEFT: *A round gilded mirror echoes its arched niche. A rusted iron candelabra adds romantic light outdoors. Plump down cushions make the window seats beneath the European-style casements hard to resist.*
RIGHT: *In the great room, formerly an artist's studio, the square beams are original; the plaster was redone with a golden yellow glow. Nearly everything else, including the windows and antique fireplace mantel, was added.*

SEDUCTIVE SCENTS

Fragrance is highly individual (that's what makes it so wonderful), but here are some favorites:

Fracas

Helmut Lang

Romance by Ralph Lauren

L'Artisan Parfumeur, which creates personal
  scents—my favorites are Santal and
  Voleur de Roses

Kiehl's Musk

Bennison scented candles

Mixing two scents to create your own; for
  example, Etro and Calvin Klein's Oil
  Essences are two collections designed to
  be worn this way

Ken Turner candles

Diptyque's Tuberose and Gardenia

Agraria potpourri

Coppertone suntan lotion

feeling is that it's all been there a long time," she says. "It took two months to get the plasterers to understand that I wanted them to create the appearance of age and water damage in the stucco outside. They thought I was crazy, but they finally did it." The interior walls were plastered with integrally colored diamond-finished stucco with a warm sandy tone in the great room and a flattering soft apricot in the bedrooms.

The rooms are decorated in a purely romantic, yet sophisticated, fashion. In the living room, faded rose bouquets on the scallop-topped curtains and softly striped summer slipcovers change over to cozy velvets and salmon chenille in winter. The master bedroom is even more dreamlike, with pale peach Fortuny bed curtains creating a sheltering cocoon, and faded Bennison rose linens on a beautiful painted Italian bed. An English chaise and standing candelabra in the adjacent dressing/sitting room, along with the stone floors and European casement windows, enhance the feeling of being secluded in a storybook castle.

The captivating interiors are only half of the story, however. Both the main house and the guest house are surrounded by lush terraced perennial gardens closer in style to English cottages than Santa Fe cactuses, thanks to the bounty of the acequia. Curving stone walls and flowering vine-covered windows and loggias create the illusion of being transported to southern France before one even enters the front door. The property also encompasses extensive vegetable gardens, orchards, and a farm that produces organic produce year-round. "Here I am working on the stock market on the twenty-ninth floor of an office building in Houston, and at the same time, I'm growing all these wonderful fruits and vegetables in New Mexico," marvels the owner.

In some ways, it's that complete disconnect between her two worlds—the high-pressured life of a globe-trotting investment banker and the peaceful isolation of her Tesuque retreat—that offers the greatest appeal. "My work is dictated by communication and technology. I didn't want any part of that when I came here," she says. In fact, she fashioned her otherworldly escape so successfully that no matter where she put her computer, it threatened to ruin the decor. So she is now building a separate home office away from the house.

In addition to the potential for time travel this seemingly centuries-old home offers, the memories it shelters are also cherished by its owners. "I think travel is so incredibly important. Everywhere you go, the things you bring back help evoke those times and places." She recently visited the remote province of Kashgar in the far west of China and brought back a Khotan rug that will inspire the design of her new office. "It makes me think of the Grand Tour and what an extraordinary experience that must have been, how people brought back all kinds of curiosities from their travels." For this homeowner, who's been on the equivalent of a lifelong Grand Tour, her magical house in New Mexico re-creates the wonder of those journeys every day.

LEFT: *The view from the newly added second-floor master bedroom stretches all the way to Colorado. Or, the Fortuny bed curtains can be drawn to screen the morning light and offer privacy.*

Isn't It Romantic?

Softly aged walls, glowing with gentle color

Tall European-style casement windows that can be opened at night and at midday to create natural air-conditioning

The softest down window-seat cushions

Authentic centuries-old French limestone floors and counters

Antiques and mementos brought back from journeys around the world

A bed enveloped in curtains that can be closed off from the rest of the world

A dressing/sitting room with a chaise longue

A bathroom sink that is nothing more than an old marble font and simple spout

Lush flowering vines overhanging and shading each window

A covered loggia to shelter large windows from the sun

A profusion of lush flowers and greenery in the midst of the desert

LEFT: *Nineteenth-century French limestone on counters and floors instantly aged the kitchen.*
TOP RIGHT: *The exterior stucco was mottled to give the appearance of age.*
BOTTOM RIGHT: *An old marble holy water font and the simplest of taps in a powder room.*

A LAYERING OF LIFETIMES

*W*hat's romantic to me," says interior designer Thomas Callaway, "is the notion of living in another time and place. The minute I drive down our road, which has a country feel about it even though it is in the city, and come through our front door, I feel completely transported out of America and into this idyllic, self-imposed dream of living in Europe." What makes the fantasy so compelling is the transformation Tom has wrought on the enchanting Cotswold-style cottage he shares with his wife, Claire, and their teenage son in Los Angeles. "When I was nineteen, I lived in Europe for a while and I was mesmerized by the centuries-old architecture everywhere. America seemed so new by comparison. I couldn't get enough, and ever since, I've been trying to create the romance of how that impressed me.

"There are so many things I like, I can't live with them all at once, so I've chosen one thing at a time," says Tom. "No matter which style I've done, each one has been an early historical period that's quite different from America now." Tom and Claire have been married almost thirty years, and their homes —and collecting focus—can be almost evenly divided into decades, or thirds. Their first home, on the East Coast, was American Federal, and they began collecting American and English antiques. Ten years later, they moved to the West Coast. "Thrilled by the Spanish influence, which was all new to me," says Tom, "we lived in a Spanish Colonial, early rancho–style home and collected Spanish *retablos* [small religious paintings] and Native American art, which I'd been collecting since high school." Their latest passion is their English-style cottage, which has inspired more English and French collecting.

What's most interesting is that Tom and Claire haven't just tossed out everything and started fresh in each of these dramatically different homes and locales. "What I found in the first move was that so many things I thought wouldn't work, looked right once we moved in," says Tom. "All our previous things have come with us—edited for space and flow, of course—and the eclectic mix creates a layering of lifetimes. It's not so purely one thing that it becomes a museum or a decorating theme. It's an amalgam of things that all mean something to us, and that makes it more personal."

A small office and bedroom were combined to create a generous library, with English oak paneling, built-in bookshelves, half-timbered walls, and diamond-leaded windows. Leather chairs, sailboat models, and antlers are romantic icons of a masculine sort.

Their current house is a stucco English-style cottage built in 1938 that had simple plaster walls and generally modest rooms when they bought it. It was the living room, with its high, timbered ceilings, leaded diamond windows, and inglenook that "spoke volumes" to Tom about what the house could be. "That room inspired the whole project, but the house did not have that old-world feeling throughout," says Tom. He set about thoroughly Anglicizing the house by covering the exterior in six different types of fieldstone for a realistically old feel; half-timbering the interior using weathered, rough wood; adding paneling and more leaded-glass windows; and combining some small rooms to create more spacious proportions and higher ceilings. What is now a refined and inviting library, paneled in English oak and lined floor to ceiling with bookshelves, was originally a small office and bedroom Tom joined into one. The timbers in the ceiling are stenciled in a William Morris pattern he adapted from the cover of an antique autograph book. The master bedroom had been a little study with a low ceiling, which he ripped out, creating a half-timbered cathedral ceiling that reaches up into what was previously the attic. In this room, he had the beams painted and added a delicate floral stencil on the plastering.

Even though the main rooms now have high ceilings, "they are still cozy and warm.

They are scaled to people, and are not massive spaces that feel cold," explains Tom. The dining room feels particularly intimate, with its small fireplace/oven built into one wall. No one would guess that this was once an exterior patio that Tom enclosed, converting what had been an outdoor barbecue into a fireplace. He covered the walls in vertical board paneling and added a leaded-glass door. The couple's overstuffed furniture (with many pieces from Tom's own furniture line, Thomas Callaway Benchworks), upholstered in a mix of leather and bargello needlepoint, aged velvet, tapestry, and paisley, and their collections of Quimper pottery, blue-and-white export porcelain, silver loving cups, American portraits, and crystal decanters—to name just a few—make the house feel as if it's been part of an English country estate for generations.

The compelling illusion continues outdoors, where Tom leveled a steep hillside jungle into a neat green yard bordered with fieldstone retaining walls and a little stone dovecote that "gives that Cotswold feeling a little push," as he puts it.

Asked to choose a favorite room, Tom answers without hesitation: "The library—because of what it looks and feels like, and also the fact that it's our media center, where my son and I watch football or Claire and I watch *Masterpiece Theater*"—no doubt carefully studying those interiors, and at the same time, having them feel cozily familiar.

RIGHT: *The rich colors, plush velvet upholstery, and architectural detail conjure the ambience of an English library very convincingly.*
FOLLOWING PAGES, CLOCKWISE FROM TOP LEFT: *The living room, with its timbered walls, rustic beams, and leaded windows, provided cues for the renovation of the rest of the house. The Soutine chair and ottoman are Thomas Callaway's own design, as is the leather and bargello-patterned settee. Tom covered the brick fireplace in plaster and wood. Note the whimsical bear andirons.*

*"Tudor style is **COZY** to start with, and the paneling*

and half timbering give it a lot of warmth*."*

LEFT: *Quimper pottery is Claire's latest collecting passion, and it fills every inch of an old cupboard from Wisconsin that Tom bought when he was in high school.*

ABOVE: *A patio became the dining room with the addition of vertical-board paneling, a leaded-glass door and skylight, and a barbecue-turned-fireplace.*

RIGHT: *The quintessentially English dining room: an ancestor portrait surrounded by mounted antlers and a silver tea service.*

Isn't It Romantic?

*Half-timbered walls, diamond-paned
leaded-glass windows, and cathedral ceilings*

*Silver trays filled with crystal decanters,
porcelain tea sets, and silver picture frames*

*Upholstery embellished with bullion, moss,
pompom fringe, and tassels, with none of it
feeling over-the-top*

*Warm, rich burgundies and golds; aged
leathers and intricate paisleys*

*A true library, with oak paneling, floor-to-
ceiling bookcases, globes, and ship models*

*A small fireplace/wood-burning oven built
into the wall of a dining room*

*A cathedral-ceiling bedroom that feels warm
and cozy, with stenciled walls and beams*

A picturesque fieldstone dovecote

*The feeling of being transported to another
time and place*

RIGHT: *Tom borrowed details from a Scottish
dovecote to create this enchanting one built
into the stone wall in his own yard.*
FAR RIGHT: *By tearing out the eight-foot ceilings in the master bedroom and opening it up
to the attic, Tom created a lofty space that still
feels cozy thanks to its stenciled walls and half-
timbered ceiling.*

Eclectic Romance

It's design that can't be categorized, that's ruled more by the spirit than the swatch. It's people who decorate according to a personal compass that isn't swayed by passing fads, and who have cultivated their own unique style. It's decorating with a passion that makes eclectic romance so compelling.

A skyline of wooden candlesticks, some from churches, some not, stand silhouetted against a window with Mexican shutters in Dianne Cash's Santa Fe home.

HOUSE OF MIRACLES

Sixteen years ago, Dianne Cash and her husband, Barry, purchased a magical home in Santa Fe that had belonged to the founders of the Santa Fe opera. Designed by "the father of Santa Fe style," John Gaw Meem, in 1947, it is nestled high on a ridge that affords 360-degree views of Santa Fe. The house boasts a sparkling vista of the city from the den and pool, a view north up the road to Taos from the breakfast room, and a panorama of the Sangre de Cristo mountains from the entry hall.

Shortly after they bought the house, Dianne learned that she had breast cancer. "It sounds odd, but I thought, 'If I die, this is where I want to be,'" she remembers. "Santa Fe is such a spiritual place. I felt so close to God and nature here." As she underwent treatment, she plunged headfirst into renovating and furnishing the house. "It gave me a great sense of purpose and hope, which really helped me get through that difficult period," says Dianne, who has now been cancer-free for fifteen years. A renovation that could have easily taken two years to complete was finished in just a year, thanks to Dianne's determination and devotion as she battled her illness. Though Dianne and Barry have since divorced, the house and its lush grounds "were truly a labor of love," she says, which they both worked on to create a retreat for their five children, who were teenagers at the time and are now grown, with families of their own.

Dianne and Barry eventually doubled the size of the house, adding a large window-wrapped den and a more intimate library, and enlarging the kitchen by converting the front porch into a breakfast room. What had been the living room became a master bedroom, and part of the adjacent garage was converted into an opulent master bath. They were determined to maintain the integrity of the original structure, adding on without disturbing existing rooms and ensuring that the whole house looks as though it's always been here. "The charming thing about Santa Fe is that it's deceiving. Houses look small, but you never know what you're going to see behind the closed doors," says Dianne,

RIGHT: *A passageway that joins the original house to a new addition features fifteen-foot-high coved plaster ceilings. Dianne replaced all the doors in the house with antiques, like this fanciful wrought-iron gate.*
FOLLOWING PAGES, TOP LEFT: *In the guest bedroom, a gossamer white lace canopy airily frames a wrought-iron bed lavished with pillows.* BOTTOM LEFT: *A dressing table is draped in an early 1800s Spanish cutwork cloth.* TOP RIGHT: *In the master bath, a carved Italian mirror crowns another feminine dressing table. The copper tub is adorned with a halo of antique French lace.* BOTTOM RIGHT: *Dianne displays her concho belts on a chair back.*

"There's a __romance__ to things once owned by others—

*the **charm** and **mystery** of another era.”*

NO-FAIL INGREDIENTS FOR ROMANCE

Candlelight and dimmer switches
Room service
Champagne
A fire in the fireplace
Music
Chocolate, caviar, oysters—or any
favorite indulgence
Bubble baths, whirlpools, or hot tubs
Handwritten notes
Fresh flowers
Driving in a convertible
The beach or the water
Flying over New York City at night
A tuxedo

which is especially true of the elaborately carved, cobalt-blue gated entrance, originally from Afghanistan, that now leads to her compound. Dianne found antique doors for every doorway in the house, shutters for many windows, and balustrades and architectural ornamentation for the portals and garden. Her talented eye is evident in the way every surface has become an artful tableau.

To say that Dianne is an avid collector is almost an understatement. In her frequent travels, she acquired Spanish Colonial, Mexican, Native American, Moroccan, Italian, and North African architectural artifacts, furnishings, artwork, and collectibles for the Santa Fe home. She has always collected textiles, including religious vestments from the seventeenth through nineteenth centuries, but here her collections also encompass santos (carved wooden statues of saints) and their silver and gold crowns, intricate silver- and tinwork, candelabras and candlesticks, Native American moccasins and tribal robes, and crosses and other forms of religious art. Even her own clothing and accessories have become collections of "wearable art." "If I'm not wearing it, it's draped over a chair or displayed on a table," Dianne says of the collection of Spanish embroidered shawls that serves as an informal divider in the master

ABOVE LEFT: *Dianne and her husband built a chapel on the property, which she has filled with antique religious vestments, santos, and other religious icons.*
LEFT: *The bisque figures of these* niños—*baby Jesus santos—are well suited to this simple plaster niche.*
RIGHT: *A door is covered with milagros, or "miracles"—charms used to pray for the healing of injuries.*

bath, or the assortment of concho belts lined up across a chair. Despite the seamless continuity between the house and its contents, "I've never gotten a house and sought out things for it," she says. "I've always been a buyer of things—whether very valuable collectibles or flea-market finds—and then I've found a place for them. I am guided simply by what appeals to me."

Over time the Cashes added gardens, a pool, a studio, and guest houses. The gratitude Dianne felt for surviving her health crisis was the impetus behind her building a chapel on the property five years ago. "I am sure the experiences I went through made me even more spiritual," she says, a grace reflected in her collections of religious art, which also embody the cultural heritage of the area. Though she is not Catholic, she appreciates "the passion and devotion evident in the handwork—in the carving of the santos, the intricacy of the silverwork. Someone made each piece individually, with great love," she says. The chapel also became an ideal venue for Dianne's collections of antique religious vestments. Their appeal to Dianne is both spiritual and historical. "Santa Fe represents four hundred years of Indian, Hispanic, and American culture," she points out. "We tried to bring all that history into the house. To me, there's a romance in past lives and the cultures they represent. I wonder how many people have used this writing desk, where they lit this candelabra, what eyes once peered through these iron gates? What did they see? There's a great romance and mystery in all that to me."

With its evocations both historical and personal, Dianne Cash's exquisite home and its enchanting setting offer a compelling tribute to the resilient romance of the spirit.

Isn't It Romantic?

Dressing tables with antique lace table skirts, silver dresser sets, and pairs of candlestick lamps that emit a soft glow

Collections of intriguing candlesticks everywhere

A lacy canopy for a copper clawfoot tub

An airy wrought-iron bed draped with gauzy lace curtains

The gleam of ornate, hand-worked silver in frames, mirrors, and candlesticks

Completely surrounding yourself with treasures from the past

Enchanting 360° views from a mountaintop

Building in centuries-old architectural artifacts found on trips abroad

TOP LEFT: *An underground sprinkler system allows Dianne to grow a lush abundance of flowers.* LEFT: *Upholstered chaises from India surround the pool, against a backdrop of native grasses.* RIGHT: *Dianne scoured sources for old doors and other architectural artifacts to create a timeless effect indoors and out.*

LOVE SHACK

*E*very beach house, especially one with the good fortune to be on the water, has an intrinsic romance, borne of the rhythmic lullaby of the ocean waves, the awe-inspiring natural beauty, and the chance to live with fewer clothes, fewer cares, warmed by the sun and caressed by the breeze. But Pamela and Bob Melet's house has a particular romance: that heady, first-love feeling, where all that's required is free for the taking—a bonfire or a starlit night or a nap on the beach embraced in your lover's arms.

The Melets' honeymoon cottage, on the easternmost tip of Long Island, in Montauk, is just such an enchanted place. Pamela had been living in Montauk for more than a decade, and every day she would drive by a community of seven small shacks on the bay, jokingly referred to as "Millionaire's Row" by the locals, which had always captivated her. One day she saw a little homemade FOR SALE sign on one of them, and she ended up buying the tumbledown one-room shack, hoping to one day restore it.

Enter Bob Melet, who as a stylist for Ralph Lauren Home was busy getting the East Hampton Polo store ready for the summer season. When he confessed to friends on staff that he was tired of dating and ready to settle down, they immediately said in unison, "Pammy!" After their first romantic

date, a picnic on the Montauk cliffs, Bob had to go away for three weeks, but Pam stayed on his mind. Most important, as someone with a collector's love of vintage style and a set designer's vision, "Bob saw what I saw in the cottage," says Pam. "A lot of other people just didn't get it."

Pamela and Bob began renovating the cottage but stayed so true to its roots that it looks like it's never been touched. While others might have tried to expand or modernize it, Pam and Bob kept it primitive—and therein lies its charm. In this tiny space, their thoughtful touches have created a rustic temple to romance: They built a platform bed so that even when they're lying down, they have an eye-level view of sunsets on the bay through the picture window. They added a small fireplace, and Bob set about concealing the surround with piles of flat, sandy-hued rocks he collected on the beach. (They have since had the stones grouted into a permanent surround topped by a mantel of driftwood.) They built a small deck onto the front of the cottage, along with a secluded area for an outdoor shower and a clawfoot tub with its own private view of the water. "There's nothing like taking a romantic shower under the stars late at night," says Pam.

Pam wanted even the appliances to fit the beach-shack aesthetic of the 1930s cot-

The guitar by the fireplace is an especially treasured find: It belonged to a Marine in WWII and was signed by every man in his division with his hometown.

tage, so she kept the original enamel gas stove and bought a working refrigerator of the same vintage from an old motel in town. Passionate flea market hunters, Bob and Pam chose every detail with care, from the vintage railroad luggage racks used as shelves beside the bed to the tin-lined wooden baker's tubs (with wheels added for easy access) that slide beneath the bed for moth-proof clothes storage. The offbeat collections—French children's espadrilles hanging by the fire, boomerangs on the deck, canoe paddles (along with two Old Town canoes) hanging from the ceiling—are all Bob's deft touches, the bounty of flea-market trips for his work.

Each detail evokes romantic memories, such as the grass skirt lining the kitchen counter, which was one of many used to skirt the tables at their wedding reception, or the beads found at the Paris flea market hanging over the entrance to their WC. The quirky, unexpected, and personally meaningful are what attract Bob and Pam, and what makes this getaway uniquely their own.

The two share an equally small apartment in New York City, and the first thing everyone asks them is: Where do you go when you fight? Pam's answer suggests that maybe small spaces are good for relationships: "We just don't fight!" Pam and Bob's cottage (and new baby!) are proof that romance can never be measured in dollars and cents and that the best things do come in small packages.

ABOVE: *A salvaged tractor seat provides an unexpected perch in the outdoor shower.*
TOP RIGHT: *Luggage racks from old railway cars hold beach reads and mementos by the bed.*
RIGHT: *One-room living on a truly small scale: The "bedroom," "living room," and kitchen are all within a step of one another.*

Isn't It Romantic?

A private outdoor shower and clawfoot tub

*A raised, built-in bed with the cozy feeling
of a camp bunk and a glorious
view of the ocean*

A fireplace framed in beach rocks

A kitchen counter wearing a grass skirt

*Bookshelves arranged as a wonderful
vignette of shared adventure, including works
by F. Scott and Zelda Fitzgerald and
Lewis and Clark, as well as* Jaws

*A vintage-style rotary phone on its own tiny
perch next to the bed*

Deck railings made from driftwood

*Traveling by canoe, then hanging it
from the ceiling*

*Found art and quirky collections no one else
would ever even think to assemble*

One-room living

TOP RIGHT: *Tin-lined baker's tubs store clothes
and other items beneath the raised platform bed.*
BOTTOM RIGHT: *Piles of flat rocks Bob has
collected on the beach form "walls" on the deck.*
FAR RIGHT: *On every surface, like this telephone
table, there's room for a few quirky pieces.
The bath is hidden behind the beads.*

GLOBAL HARMONY

*S*anta Fe casts a magical spell on many of its visitors. For some, like Nancy and Jack, the pull is so strong they decide to put down roots. "There's something special about this place—the landscape, the culture, the spiritual feeling here," says Nancy. "I actually think I've lived here in another life. I feel more at home in the Southwest desert and mountains than I do in my native Indiana."

Nancy is an avid antiques collector and designer who works with a gallery in Scottsdale, Arizona, but she spent most of her career as a psychotherapist. Though the two might not seem related, she finds interior design is often influenced by psychology and relationship dynamics. "I thought I was getting away from therapy, but in reality, I was just adding another specialty," she jokes.

Nancy, often accompanied by her husband, is constantly on the prowl for antiques for both her clients and herself. "I often buy things not knowing where they are going to land," she says. Yet after thirty-five years of visiting and ten years of renting in Santa Fe, "when I finally found this house, everything just seemed to know where it belonged." She collects a lot of Spanish Colonial furniture and architectural artifacts, but in fact there

Nancy topped part of a massive column that came from the mansion of a New York lumber magnate with stone to create her dining table. The chest is Spanish, from the late 1800s.

are Italian, French, Indian, Indonesian, and early-American pieces all living in global harmony in this house, united by Nancy's discerning eye and well suited to the rich mix of cultures (Spanish, Mexican, Native American) that has always characterized Santa Fe.

This small adobe house in the historic district was originally a holding pen for livestock in the mid-1800s, then evolved into a three-bedroom bunkhouse with a kitchen and portal (small porch). A previous owner added a living room and a semienclosed porch. Nancy's renovations were designed simply to restore the house to its native state. She had all the adobe walls replastered and the painted vigas and beams sandblasted back to natural wood. It was too expensive to tear up the living room floor of red brick laid in sand, so she had an artist stain it using layers of red, green, and black, so it now looks like a floor that has naturally deepened in color over time.

Nancy has turned her home into a showcase for an intriguing mix of collections, including elaborate Indonesian chests, richly colored Indian textiles, carved Spanish furniture, and Russian icons, without allowing them to overpower the space. "Even though there are a lot of beautiful things here, I wanted the house to be comfortable and user-friendly," she says. White, washed-linen slipcovered sofas in the living room are "the most comfortable sofas you'll ever sit on, which makes them great for a vacation home," says Nancy. She embellishes them with family-heirloom lace tablecloths laid

More architectural alchemy: Nancy removed sliding glass doors, had an alcove built for the TV and stereo, and fronted it with antique carved Peruvian doors from the Santa Fe flea market.

161

Isn't It Romantic?

A fireplace in the bedroom and bath

Draping a lacy antique tablecloth across the back of a simple white sofa

Replacing standard doors with weathered antique ones, and replacing pulls with antique hardware

Candlelit, colored-glass Moroccan lanterns

Looking at surfaces and elements in your home as a potential canvas for artistic expression—your own or others'

Incorporating exotic and antique textiles into your home

Using antique chests instead of standard vanities in the bath

Displaying a rack of beautiful antique hand towels in the bath

TOP LEFT: *In a master bedroom with the luxury of its own kiva, a carved plaque, probably Spanish, serves as a headboard of sorts.*
LEFT: *Fringed and embroidered hand towels, many of them antique, are displayed on a textile rod in the master bath.*
TOP RIGHT: *There is even a fireplace in the master bath, where intricately carved grain chests have artisan-made tile backsplashes to match.*
RIGHT: *Old Indian camel covers, now lined in silk taffeta, serve as bedspreads in the guest room.*

CARRYING A TORCH

Almost any album of these greats—old and new—will do:

Tony Bennett	Diana Krall
Ray Charles	Helen Merrill
Patsy Cline	Anita O'Day
Nat King Cole	Nina Simone
Ella Fitzgerald	Frank Sinatra
Billie Holiday	Sarah Vaughan
Norah Jones	Dinah Washington

across the back, much the way she stylishly layers clothes and mixes jewelry. And not everything in her house has an exotic provenance: All the window treatments are inexpensive lace panels from Wal-Mart.

Nancy looks upon even everyday needs and functional demands as an opportunity for artistic expression and a chance to collaborate with talented artisans. The vanities in the bathrooms are carved and painted grain chests from Indonesia and India, and Nancy commissioned Taos ceramicist Jill Rounds to make handmade tiles for the backsplash that copy the styling of the chests almost exactly. Textile artist Chris Galusha hand-stenciled the suede dining chairs with gold-leaf patterns and made many of the hand-punched leather and parchment lampshades.

Nancy balances the complexity of the art and antiques by keeping the backgrounds simple, clean, and soothing—white adobe walls, white upholstery, pale beamed ceilings, and neutral tile and brick floors. Like a good hostess, she has an instinctive talent for knowing which "guests" can play a starring role and which need to take a backseat.

With a fragrant piñon-wood fire burning in the kiva, the glow of candlelight from tiny votives and statuesque candelabras, the light filtering through the pierced lampshades, and even the stars in the sky, it's not hard to see why Santa Fe is considered one of the most romantic spots in the world.

ABOVE: *Nancy used whimsical fragments of trim from old chests to enliven shelves she built herself in the kitchen.*
RIGHT: *Canvas shades the portal during the day, and at night, an eighteenth-century Moroccan lantern illuminates it. Old French folding chairs take up minimal space on the small patio.*

A LIFETIME'S LOVE

*J*olie Kelter and Michael Malcé met through the antiques business thirty-one years ago. In a testament to their compatibility, they are still working and living together more than three decades later. "We're partners in a lot of ways," Michael says sweetly. He and Jolie are dealers specializing in American folk art in Manhattan, but almost every weekend and for the entire month of July, they escape to Long Island's East End to a Victorian farmhouse built in 1896. There, the couple's quirky, whimsical taste takes hold in rooms organized around themes such as swimming and boating (inspired by their seaside location) or colorful PlaySkool toys of the 1930s

and '40s. In this way, their house—room by room, and chapter by chapter—reads like the biography of a wonderful shared life together.

The nine-room house has a pair of sitting rooms, one of which focuses on an aquatic theme, not with traditional nautical accents like pond yachts and life buoys, but in the eclectic Kelter-Malcé manner that includes, for instance, a truly remarkable bathing cap collection. One of several hooked rugs hanging on the wall was made by the artisan Steven Anderson from a photograph taken of a teenage Jolie on the beach in a bikini, which Michael commissioned and gave her as a gift. There are sailboat and swimmer

LEFT: *A terrace fashioned from railroad ties is home to a long table surrounded by a rainbow of 1940s metal pool chairs and set with enamel picnicware.*
ABOVE: *Thick stands of beach grass shelter the pool for privacy.*

paintings, nautical blue-and-white-stripe mattress-ticking pillows, and even maple furniture from the 1920s that incorporates painted cartouches of fish.

In every nook and cranny, it seems, is an unexpected and thoroughly engaging collection, from the striped dime-store glasses complemented by a "bouquet" of similarly striped Pick-Up sticks to marble and glass eggs made for nesting hens and for Easter decorations. One of the guest bedrooms is home to a winsome primary-colored collection of early PlaySkool toys, which find a graphic equivalent in an enamel hotel dresser from the 1920s by industrial designer Norman Bel Geddes, and even a Mondrian-patterned needlepoint pillow. Jolie and Michael have the inspired eye to see the charm in a fan of old croquet mallets or a Bakelite radio as a lamp base. It is clear they enjoy collecting and selling antiques, not so much for profit but for passion.

As befits a summer home, the outdoors has its attractions as well, among them a seductive pool framed by huge, lush sprays of beach grass and decking with the feel of tide-tumbled driftwood. On the screened porch, "the scent of wild honeysuckle fills the air, with the sound of crickets and tree frogs in

TOP LEFT: *Vintage mattress ticking on pillows adds a nautical accent to 1920s furniture in a living room.*
LEFT: *French woven rope chairs, a tabletop inlaid with butterflies, and a lamp base made from a Bakelite radio: Quirky finds abound in the Kelter-Malcé home.*
TOP RIGHT: *The colors and ebullience of old wooden PlaySkool toys inspired this guest room.*
RIGHT: *An advertising display featuring a trio of bathers holds up a spray of bright bathing caps.*

Isn't It Romantic?

An arbor shaded by a canopy of grapevines

A pool hidden by sprays of beach grasses

Sensual pleasures—the scent of wild honeysuckle, the chirping of crickets

A sense of humor and a sense of whimsy

Pieces chosen and saved for sentiment rather than investment

THE SEXIEST CARS

The makeout cars of your youth are always sexy, along with these racy models:

'64 black Thunderbird
Mazda Miata
BMW Z8 convertible
Jaguar XKE Roadster
Vintage pickup truck
Bathtub Porsche 356
'59 Corvette
1960s Mustang convertible

the background," says Michael. When he and Jolie bought the house five years ago, there was a massive, tangled pile of grapevines outside. Carpenter Jeffrey Cayle jacked up the morass of vines, some as thick as a foot at the base (they date from the 1890s), then built a 100-foot-long grape arbor beneath them. The grapes have now filled out the arbor nicely, and Jolie and Michael have an ample crop to eat and share with the birds; they even make grape juice. "It's a wonderful spot in summer," says Michael. "It's cool and shady, and we often eat out there." Next to it is an old shingled building that was the original Bridgehampton schoolhouse. Now, confesses Michael, it is "a giant closet, filled with 'the things you're going to fix tomorrow, the mistakes you've made, all the chairs with three legs.'" Old chicken coops house a playroom/pool house with a Ping-Pong table and a small guest house with a bedroom and bath. "We're popular in the summertime," Michael says; he and Jolie have four children between them and five grandbabies. And while they love their family and the setting, they are "things" people, he says. "We love learning the history of a piece, looking at it in different ways, and the pleasure of living with it," says Michael. In their home, every picture and every piece recounts a love story that only gets better with each telling.

ABOVE: *In the playroom, a collection of birch-bark frames holds family photographs.*
RIGHT: *Colorfully striped glasses once sold in the five-and-ten and 1920s English luncheon china share a tapering cupboard in the dining room.*
FOLLOWING PAGES: *The shingled outbuilding now wreathed in flowers was the first Bridge-hampton schoolhouse.*

SOUL MATES

y love affair with Santa Fe began twenty-five years ago, when I first started visiting this incredible place. It only deepened when I met my husband, Reg, here seven years ago, and has continued to grow as we've shared a home. It starts the minute I step off the plane in Albuquerque and begin driving to Santa Fe. I'm constantly struck by the beauty of this area, what I think of as the "Georgia O'Keeffe" landscape—big, puffy white clouds in a crystal-blue sky; the clean, clear light; the wide-open space, the beauty of the high desert at an altitude of 7,000 feet.

Because of my work as creative director for *Country Home* magazine, I spend at least two weeks each month in Des Moines, Iowa, and much of the rest of the time traveling. Reg is based in Phoenix, so our tiny getaway home in Santa Fe is really our only common ground. While it's hard being apart (though cell phones, e-mail, and faxes make it easier), the wonderful thing about our arrangement

is that it's always a honeymoon when we're together. I make a special effort not to talk on the phone and not to succumb to my usual tendency to clean up and organize everything, and just enjoy Reg's company. We're at a point in our lives where we've each finished raising our families and we can focus on each other. We have time to be romantic, and we make the most of it.

Our nineteenth-century adobe house in the old Barrio section of Santa Fe is just 850 square feet, with one bedroom. We chose a small house so it would require minimal maintenance while we're away. We also bought the lot next door and we've planted a lavender garden that fills our property with wonderful fragrance and color. We planted the lavender in four squares, each with a pine tree in the center, so that in the winter, when the lavender is gone, there's still the scent of pine. I also love the scent of the piñon, or pine wood, we use as firewood—it's heavenly.

TOP LEFT: *Cinco greets visitors at the gates to the terrace.*
LEFT: *A big octagonal twig table invites guests to pull up a chair. Candles and even a sparkler in a champagne bottle make the occasion a little more festive.*
FOLLOWING PAGES: *Against a bleached backdrop of adobe walls and slipcovered couches, Navajo blankets, leopard pillows, and Mexican silver come to the fore.*

Everything in this house is about comfort and ease. There is always a bottle of champagne in the refrigerator and nuts, olives, and cheeses on hand in case people drop by. I think that a bar table or tray says welcome, too, and I love setting one up with a mix of silver cups, wicker-wrapped bottles, and votive candles.

The interior design elements are the same ones I've used in nearly all of my homes—white-slipcovered sofas with leopard-print, paisley, serape, and Navajo-blanket pillows and lots of mirrors and big wicker baskets; my old pine and painted country furniture—and then I layer on my collections. The incredibly rich cultural history of Santa Fe has inspired me to collect the primitive religious art and icons that are so prevalent in this area and in Mexico, including santos (statues of saints), crosses, and *milagros* (sacred charms offered as prayers for mira-

cles). Candles, from dime-store votives to elegant silver candelabras, work well with these collections and add to the soulful quality I find so unique to Santa Fe.

My philosophy of turning storage into display works wonderfully in a small house. There are necklaces on our old Italian headboard and on small heart-shaped nails in the bathroom. I enjoy seeing my treasures every day rather than storing them out of sight.

I think romantic decorating comes from texture—the feel of velvet or cashmere—and color, which can be soft and soothing or strong and sexy. Just as important are the things you love, like souvenirs of trips that bring back wonderful memories. Romance is also about simple things—the sky, the moon, the breeze, having people over for a barbecue. It's about sitting back and saying, "This is the life!" Romance is all about magic, and you can never have too much of it!

ABOVE: *I always like to have an informal bar set up for entertaining. It can be as simple as a tray of decanters or bottles, bowls of lemons and limes, and glasses.*
RIGHT: *Black-and-white photographs in simple black frames, like these pictures of Georgia O'Keeffe and other Santa Fe icons, are simultaneously modern and timeless.*

Rules for Romance

Scale matters. When rooms, homes, and beds get too big, they lose their charm. Queen-size is romantic; king is not.

The more layers—more pillows, more blankets—the softer and more romantic the look.

Candles, fresh flowers, and framed photographs of family and friends make a home feel lived in.

Details make something special and romantic. Own things that you would feel compelled to save if there was a fire.

Dimmers are essential. When you're decorating and choosing paint colors, think about how things will look at night.

Clutter is an instant romance-killer. Use wicker baskets, attractive boxes, peg racks, and shelves to help organize, corral, and conceal all the odds and ends of daily life.

Display objects that make you smile—photographs, special gifts, funny cards—in plain sight where you can enjoy them every day.

LEFT: *Open storage: Enjoy your jewelry by keeping it out in a basket or bowl. Or hang necklaces, scarves, or handbags from doorknobs or peg racks.*
TOP RIGHT: *Turquoise and coral necklaces hang from my carved Italian headboard.*
RIGHT: *Make your bed a haven: Indulge in a pillow-top mattress, down pillows, and beautiful bed linens.*

MARY'S TOP TEN ROMANTIC COLLECTIBLES

1. Colored glass (wineglasses, tumblers, votives) instead of clear.
2. Vintage ceramic vases in a mix of sizes and shapes.
3. Mercury glass for the gleam of silver with the extra reflection of glass.
4. Rhinestone jewelry (from $10 to $100) to pin on a jean jacket, belt loop, the lapel of a black suit, or a hat.
5. Silver candelabra with drippy candles. Two are always better than one.
6. Silver-plate trays and bowls. I use them in the bath, for pillar candles on a coffee table, for holding keys on a hall table, or for serving drinks or nuts.
7. Teddy bears, a sentimental link to your inner child.
8. Necklaces, whether old pearls, jewel-like beads, or modern silver, displayed on hooks, candelabra, mirrors, doorknobs, or headboards.
9. Old-fashioned glassware—gold-rimmed, cut-crystal, or simple jelly glasses—for everyday use.
10. Vintage Christmas ornaments like the ones you remember from childhood. They just don't make them like that anymore.

RIGHT: *Ornate Mexican silver frames, a charming primitive statue, and a cluster of roses form a vignette in the bedroom.*

FAR RIGHT: *A basket of cowboy hats (mine and Reg's) stands at the ready by the door, which has an ornate saddlebag looped on top.*

ROMANCE A TO Z

Try any—or many—of these no-fail ingredients to instantly raise the romance and charm quotient of your home.

arbors. Laden with wisteria, climbing roses, clematis, or even grapes, an arbor (or pergola) is the romantic's alternative to SPF 45. Add one to shade your terrace or any outdoor space and create another room—and another world. Luxuriate in its feeling of shelter, privacy, and enclosure, the way it dramatically frames an area for dining and adds a fragrant perfume to summer evenings.

architectural elements. Consider them character builders for your home: stately columns, paneled walls, and elegant mantels; satisfyingly deep crown moldings and baseboards, whether simple or ornate; built-in bookshelves, china cupboards, and niches. Any or all add a sense of uniqueness, permanence, and charm to your home.

Aubusson carpets. Madame de Pompadour was one of their first customers; need we say more? The soft colors and feminine motifs of these flat-woven rugs, patterned with full-blown flowers and flourishes, are about as romantic as a carpet can get.

balconies. Ever since Romeo wooed Juliet as she stood on her balcony, these have added charm and a life outside the home to upper-story rooms. Fill a small one to overflowing with flowering blossoms, or slip a pair of chairs and a tiny table onto a larger balcony

for stargazing, sunrise watching, or champagne sipping al fresco.

beadboard. Sometimes referred to as wainscoting, usually painted white, and originally used in humble farmhouses, beadboard is paneling made chic. It is now used (and perhaps overused) in multimillion-dollar homes as shorthand for country or vintage charm in kitchens, bathrooms, and other informal rooms, but we're still not tired of its simple, distinctive character.

books. Think of them as an aphrodisiac for the mind. To a bibliophile or lover of literature, there is probably nothing more romantic than books: shelves filled with books, tables stacked with books, whole rooms lined in books, private libraries to get lost in. Perusing the titles on someone's shelves provides clues to his or her passions, intellectual curiosity, and worldliness (unless, of course, the books are old  leather volumes bought just for show).

butler's trays and bar tables. Setting up a bar is an inviting gesture that says, "Make yourself at home." Home to all those wonderful accoutrements of the bar—silver martini shakers, wicker-wrapped bottles, crystal decanters, tortoise or horn cups filled with drink stirrers, cocktail picks, matches, small bowls filled with olives and salted nuts—in short, a party to go.

candles. Much has been made of the importance of candlelight throughout this book. Suffice it to say there is no simpler, less

expensive, or more readily available route to romance than candles. Candlelight will hide a multitude of sins, including cobwebs, wrinkles (on faces and fabrics), and barely furnished or overly cluttered rooms, and put the focus on the sparkle in everyone's eyes and smile. It is warm, it is immensely flattering, and it is evocative. Whenever you're entertaining (but also when you are alone), turn off or dim the lights, and rely on candlelight to illuminate the room. The right (not overdone) scent adds to the seduction.

canopy beds. For both young girls dreaming of fairy tales and grown-up women seeking shelter from the storm, canopy beds fulfill a long-held vision of romance. Even a modernist can appreciate the beauty of a simple drape of fabric swept across the top of a clean-lined tester, while the true romantic might crave the lavish effect of lined curtains completely enveloping the bed.

cashmere. Is there any fabric more luxurious than the silky, gossamer embrace of cashmere? A cashmere throw or blanket is a well-

worth-it indulgence, adding warmth without weight, as well as luscious color.

ceiling fans. Why not replace the intrusive hum of the modern-day air-conditioner with the soft whir or click-click rhythm of a ceiling fan as it gently swishes air through a room? Ceiling fans recall slow, languid afternoons in New Orleans, or sultry nights in Casablanca.

chaise longues. The chaise is the idea of relaxation translated into form, perfect for curling up—or stretching out—with a book to read or a cup of tea. Because it often sits on its own, it has a delicious air of solitude and leisure. Every home should have a chaise—the feminine equivalent of a recliner—especially in the bedroom.

chandeliers. What ceiling fans are to air-conditioners, chandeliers are to lamps—the very embodiment of romance. Whether dripping with crystals or glass beads, or simply wrought from iron, they have long been the most elegant way to light a room. The most romantic chandeliers are lit with candles: Sure, they require more work, but they reward the effort with incredibly sensual light.

clawfoot tubs. Long before soaking tubs and whirlpools, old-fashioned clawfoot tubs best represented the ideal of a long, luxurious bath. When they are deep enough to be fully submerged in and are freestanding (not combined with a shower),

pampering, rather than efficiency, is emphasized. They're still the prettiest way to rub-a-dub-dub.

dressing tables. Remnants of a bygone era, when women had time to primp in front of the mirror, dressing tables are due for a comeback. They are seductively feminine, and the way they create a private sanctuary within a bedroom or bath is a wonderfully worthwhile luxury women should reclaim.

European square pillows. These 26-inch-square tall, stately pillows turn ordinary beds into extraordinary ones, like those you see in catalogs and magazines. They add height to the standard silhouette of pillows on a bed and provide another canvas for pattern or texture.

feather beds. Feel as entitled as a fairy-tale princess: Sleeping on a feather bed is like floating on top of a fluffy cloud. Slipped between the fitted sheet and mattress, this downy quilt warms, cushions, and coddles all at once.

fireplaces. As it has done since prehistoric times, a fire draws us in, inviting us to bask in its halo, and warming us through to our very bones. To purists, the most romantic fire is a wood fire, but the modern convenience of a gas-lit fire that can be turned on and off with the flick of a switch certainly has its advantages, especially in the bedroom. (Who wants to jump out of bed to tend the fire?) Simply put, a romantic must-have.

floral prints. Whether lush vintage blossoms on bark cloth or delicate bouquets on English chintz, floral fabrics are the cheering two-dimensional equivalent of a dozen roses from your lover, or a beautiful perennial garden blooming year-round. And you needn't go overboard—a few flowery pillows in an otherwise simple room will satisfy your need for beauty without making the man in your life feel like his masculinity's been taken hostage.

fragrance. Just as you probably have a favorite perfume, your home should have a signature fragrance. And like yours, the scent can change with the season or occasion— lily of the valley for spring, tuberose for summer, pine or a hint of cinnamon and orange for winter. Many designers and fragrance houses make wonderful scented candles for the home. Try them out until you find one you love, then use it in the evening or whenever you entertain for another layer of sensory appeal.

French doors. Instant therapy for light-starved rooms, a pair of glass-paned doors invites in sunlight and creates a sense of connection with the outdoors. French doors are an elegant way to update any ground-level room, but beware the obviously fake snap-in mullions. Splurge for true divided lights!

fresh flowers. A quick flip through any home magazine will reveal that flowers are a stylist's first line of defense in transforming a room. But why do so many of us indulge in fresh flowers only when company is coming? Affordable fresh flowers are now available at grocery stores, city bodegas, and farm stands, not to mention in your own backyard garden. Treat yourself—and your home—to a simple single-flower bouquet (or two) every week—you're worth it! To get the most bang for your buck, look for large flowers, like hydrangeas, that also dry beautifully; long-lasting flowering plants such as orchids; flowering branches for big impact; or bulbs you can force on your own. Even a small flat of grass brings color and life to a room.

fringe. The swish of a sofa's deep bullion fringe brushing the floor, the sway of a halo of fringe framing a pillow make soft furnishings feel a little more lush, a little more feminine. These are the "fringe" benefits of putting thought into the custom details that make your home one of a kind.

gables and dormers. Before modern architecture flattened houses into square boxes, sloping roofs—and their gables, eaves, and dormers—created attic rooms with charming nooks and crannies. Perhaps they're not as economical a use of space, but they certainly have more personality—and they often create the perfect cubby in which to tuck a window seat, dressing table, writing desk, or bed.

gardens. Gardens, of course, are a topic worthy of their own book. But it is hard to imagine any garden that is not in some way romantic, and any home or patch of grass that would not be improved by a garden. Think beyond zinnias and impatiens: If you're not much of a green thumb, go for old-fashioned flowering shrubs such as peonies, lilacs, and hydrangeas that will bloom without a lot of effort on your part. But there are also many easy-to-grow perennials and annuals, even roses (perhaps the epitome of romance), that reward minimal

labor with lush blossoms, sweet fragrance, and endless pleasure.

hammocks. These are leisure defined: a place devoted to idle lounging, lulled by the breeze, shaded by leafy branches. A hammock in a yard is an invitation to relaxation: Just looking at it can lower your blood pressure—but climbing in is even better. Padded ones offer more comfort, but simple rope nets please purists.

hurricane lanterns and oil lamps. Even more than candles, these suggest the romance of a bygone era of sailing ships and life before electricity. The flickering flame, sheltered from the breeze by a shell of glass, lends the perfect intimacy to an outdoor dinner or cocktails on the deck, and the stylish large-scale, simple hurricanes now widely available look equally chic indoors.

lace. Perhaps it's the peekaboo aspect of lace—what it reveals and what it doesn't—that makes it so romantic. Or the fact that it is delicate, fragile, beautifully wrought (at one time all by hand), and usually white. It softens edges with a ruffle of femininity, and lends a touch of romance to even the sparest of forms. While lace can become a cliché, most of the time it offers pure old-fashioned charm.

leather. Whether on the body or in the home, leather is more than romantic; it's downright sexy. Besides the fact that it looks and feels great, it also lasts forever, only gaining in beauty as it ages—witness the ubiquitous quest to replicate the perfect vintage leather club chair that has been worn just so.

leopard print. Answer your personal call of the wild, soothe your savage soul, reveal the animal in you with a touch of leopard. Leopard prints are surprisingly good mixers, fitting in as easily with paisleys and florals as with velvet and leather. Throw a leopard footstool or shams into the mix for a look that's instantly up-to-date and surprisingly timeless.

memory boards. A prettier version of the bulletin board, memory boards are padded and covered in fabric, then crisscrossed with a lattice of ribbon, so that you can casually tuck in a changing display of favorite photos, invitations, inspiring images, and gentle reminders without the savagery of thumbtack holes. Think of the resulting collage as an ever-changing visual diary or sentimental snapshot of your day-to-day life.

mirrors. One could joke that only narcissists find mirrors romantic, but in truth mirrors

work decorating magic. They reflect light, whether it's natural light or the glow of candlelight. They're also generally more affordable than paintings. If you can find a great frame at a flea market (it may be surrounding a lousy painting), have it fitted with a mirror for instant art.

mosquito netting. This is one example of something utterly utilitarian (and very inexpensive) turned unabashedly romantic. You don't need to be sleeping in the tropics to drape your bed in a cloud of mosquito netting (hung from a hook in the ceiling) for the most sensuous, sheer, and simple canopy imaginable.

outdoor showers. Anyone who has ever enjoyed the privilege of a showering outdoors at a beach house knows how sexy it can be to be completely naked in the fresh air, feeling the warmth of the water against the slight chill in the air (or vice versa—a cooling shower on a steamy day or night), sheltered by the privacy of a rustic wooden enclosure. Even better à deux, of course. Just be careful not to get your towel wet—or stolen!

patina. If only our faces were treated as charitably as our furniture, appreciated for their aging and character marks. Well-worn, peeling-paint, patinated surfaces are romantic because they speak of generations past, of the beauty in imperfection, of a life well lived. But beware faux aging that is too obvious or poorly executed—better to come by wear and tear authentically.

pedestal sinks. These are certainly not in vogue because they are practical—for example, you can't hide your toiletries beneath them. But there is no doubt that a sculptural porcelain pedestal sink is more beautiful than the typical boxy vanity with a sink dropped in. So find a pretty cupboard, glass shelves, or generous medicine cabinet in which to stash the stuff that seems to accumulate and indulge in one or a pair of pedestal sinks.

photographs. What are more personal and meaningful possessions than photographs? Moments frozen in time from our past, mementos of the people who are most important to us—they're part of the soul of our homes. Keep them out where you can enjoy them, whether they are framed and grouped on walls or tabletops or just piled in a basket for browsing, and update them frequently.

picket fences. There is something neat and tidy and charming about a white picket fence across the front of a house—if it's the right kind of house —and it's especially romantic if there are roses spilling over it, or clumps of daffodils clustered at its base. Don't overlook the details—a pretty garden gate or arched arbor, nicely wrought fence posts and caps.

plantation shutters. These wide, louvered shutters are used in the tropics and the South to shelter houses from the sun while allowing air to circulate. In hot climes, they might be hung in window and door openings in lieu of glass, and they could also be closed up and battened down in a storm. The clean, architectural effect of shutters, with their wide (two-inch) wooden slats, whether in island mahogany or painted wood, has a stylish, sultry elegance in any climate.

pools. Late-night skinny-dipping, peaceful floating, cocktails by the pool, bikini-clad bodies drying in the sun—let us count the many ways in which a pool inspires romance. Just the vision of that shimmering, translucent rectangle of turquoise is cooling, not to mention how luxurious it is to have a pool to call one's own.

porches, verandas, porticos, and galleries. What you call a porch may depend on where you live, but it doesn't change how wonderful it is to sit on, shaded from the sun (or enjoying the evening), taking in the breeze, slowing down the pace of life to the rhythm of a rocking chair or glider. The rise of the automobile, the backyard patio, and the ranch house spelled an unfortunate demise of the porch, but in recent years, people have thankfully come to appreciate its old-fashioned charms once again.

roses. A rose is a rose, and if it is lush and full, garden-grown, with a heady fragrance, in creamy white, the palest blush of pink, a rich seductive red, or any number of other luscious hues, there is really no other flower that can compete as a symbol of romance. There are plenty of roses that are easy to grow, but if your green thumb is easily pricked by thorns, or your garden's not in season, roses are among the most readily available and well-priced cut flowers you can buy.

sailboat models. Whether pond yachts (miniature sailboats designed to be sailed on ponds), or models of authentic sailboats, these offer a winsome, salt-tinged reminder of the romance of life on the water.

screen doors (wooden). Another sound that seems to be disappearing as more homes succumb to central air-conditioning is the slap of a screen door—in a house with children, an all-day-long rhythm—and the pleasure of a breeze. If you have an aluminum screen door, consider replacing it with a wooden one. Some have Victorian trim; others are simple and humble, as a screen door is meant to be.

screened porches and sleeping porches. A screened porch offers the pleasure of being outdoors with protection from pests as well as inclement weather—it's particularly romantic to dine on a candlelit screened porch at night in the rain. Sleeping porches—unheated rooms, usually on a second floor, lined in glass or screened windows—offer a similarly sheltered way to sleep with the restorative tonic of cool, fresh air. They were popular in lake and mountain retreats in the pre–AC early 1900s, but they are still a wonderful and romantic addition, particularly to a summer house.

shells. These talismans of the sea are free for the taking and, once home, serve as evocative mementos of summer. They might be gathered in a bowl, lined up in a frieze on a mantel or window sash, hung randomly from a sheer curtain, glued to thumbtacks on a bulletin board—the possibilities are almost as varied as the shells themselves.

silver. The soft, reflective luster of silver suggests treasured heirlooms and an appreciation for the finer things in life. The fact that it tarnishes actually increases its appeal to people who consider polishing a labor of love and who relish the way a little tarnish emphasizes the fine detail in a pattern.

slipper chairs. These armless, skirted chairs with their regal posture and soft curves are

the ideal boudoir chair, scaled to fit the feminine form perfectly and easily slip beneath a dressing table or writing desk.

snuggly sofas. No matter how fine your antiques or how modern your decor, a deep, plush, sink-in-soft sofa is a must in any room in which you spend a lot of time. While you don't have to go shabby-chic oversize, make sure your sofa is roomy and comfy enough to lie down and read, nap, or snuggle with a loved one. Invest in a quality sofa, and then you can just slipcover or reupholster it as your tastes or decor change.

sunrooms and conservatories. If it's true that sunlight elevates your mood, conservatories can be considered Prozac for the home—especially in the chilly midst of winter. Whether you fill yours with plants and flowers, or just relish it as a haven for reading or dining, these rooms, once much favored by the Victorians, are enjoying a well-earned revival.

toile. From eighteenth-century France, where these richly detailed scenic fabrics were first designed and printed; to the twentieth-century English drawing rooms where they became synonymous with good taste; to today, when this once staid pattern is being splashed on everything from tote bags to umbrellas, toile has a timeless appeal. It's especially romantic in a bedroom, used wall-to-wall on bed linens, wallpaper, curtains—or add just a few judicious touches, like pretty toile-covered boxes, for a feminine flourish.

tortoiseshell. Of course, real tortoiseshell is no longer PC (though it makes for highly sought-after antiques), but well-done faux tortoise is still a sophisticated choice for accessories such as decorative boxes, picture frames, and cups. The hint of exotic animal pattern, the rich dappled amber hue, and its slight translucency make it a classy complement to silver, wicker, and mahogany on a bar, dresser, or tabletop.

trellises. Turn a bare wall into a backdrop of flowers and you'll make any outdoor space feel more secluded and romantic. A support system for roses, clematis, honeysuckle, and other climbers, trellises are also aesthetically appealing in their own right, bringing architectural structure to a garden or embellishment to a home.

wicker. The natural, hand-woven texture, honeyed hue, and tactile quality of wicker make it infinitely more appealing than plastic when you want to de-clutter. Big wicker bins can hold catalogs, laundry, or recycling; shallow wicker trays can corral papers on a desk or condiments in the kitchen; and wicker baskets lined up on shelves can organize almost anything.

widow's walks. When a ship captain was out at sea, his wife could ascend to this balustraded platform, which crowns many Colonial and Greek Revival seaport houses, to search for his ship. That some women waited in vain for their husband's return (hence the name) only makes this distinctive architectural feature all the more heart-rending.

window seats. Curled up like a cat on a plump cushion, able to leisurely survey the world outside the window or read a good book— window seats invite such wonderful fantasy. They are a good use of wasted dormer space, especially if the seat lifts up to offer storage; a space-saving option for kitchen seating and a fun addition in kids' rooms. Make them low and wide enough to be comfortable, with a thick, soft cushion and throw pillows large and firm enough to prop up your back, and then actually use them!

wooden blinds. Light filtering through wooden slats has a seductive film-noir connotation. And wooden blinds are so much more appealing, both aesthetically and tactilely, than the aluminum or plastic mini-blinds so widely in use. There are an abundance of stained or painted finishes and colored or decorative cloth tapes to choose from.

zebra prints. Even more dramatic than other animal prints, zebra patterns are best used in small doses, but their bold graphic impact and black-and-white simplicity make them all the more compelling today.

RESOURCES

ALABAMA

The Antique Store
127 Main Street West
Hartselle, AL 35640
256-773-5620
Classic American country
antiques such as furniture,
quilts, linens, and treenware,
reproduction painted furniture,
and bench-made Windsor
chairs.

ARIZONA

Bates Collection
7034 Main Street
Scottsdale, AZ 85251
480-970-3025
www.batescollection.com
Spanish Colonial antiques,
religious artifacts, architectural
elements, unique books, and
pottery.

The Brass Armadillo
12419 North 28th Drive
Interstate 17,
    north of Cactus Road
Phoenix, AZ 85029
888-942-0030
This 40,000-square-foot mall
hosts close to 600 dealers of
antiques and collectibles.

Colonial Frontiers
244 South Park Avenue
Tucson, AZ 85719
520-622-7400
Antique furniture and folk art
from around the world.

Desert Vintage & Costume
636 North 4th Avenue
Tucson, AZ 85705
520-620-1570
Men's and women's vintage
clothing, vintage and antique
textiles, accessories, jewelry, and
period costumes.

**John C. Hill—Antique Indian
Art Gallery**
6962 East 1st Avenue,
    Suite 104
Scottsdale, AZ 85251
480-946-2910
All types of old American
Indian arts and crafts, especially
Southwest historic Pueblo pot-
tery, Navajo rugs and blankets,
baskets, and old Indian jewelry.

Morning Star Antiques
2000 East Speedway
Tucson, AZ 85719
520-881-3060
www.morningstartraders.com
A large inventory of quality
Spanish Colonial, Italian,
French, and Mexican period
furniture from the 17th, 18th,
and 19th centuries.

Morning Star Traders
2020 East Speedway
Tucson, AZ 85719
520-881-2112
www.morningstartraders.com
The finest quality Southwestern
new and antique American
Indian arts, including old pawn
jewelry, Navajo rugs, baskets,
and pottery.

CALIFORNIA

Alabaster
597 Hayes Street
San Francisco, CA 94102
415-558-0482
www.alabastersf.com
Eclectic antiques such as
alabaster, hotel silver, cake
stands, white ironstone, Venetian mirrors and chandeliers,
French ivory, and mercury glass.

Alla Prima
539 Hayes Street
San Francisco, CA 94102
415-864-8180

1420 Grant Avenue
San Francisco, CA 94113
415-397-4077

www.allaprima.net
All locations specialize in European lingerie and swimwear.

American Garage Antiques
7934 West 3rd Street
Los Angeles, CA 90048
323-658-3424
Nineteenth-century American
country painted furniture, folk
art, and rustic and lodge
furnishings.

Barclay Butera L.A.
169 North La Brea
Los Angeles, CA 90036
(323) 634-0200
Casual, elegant, tailored
furniture by Barclay Butera,
Ralph Lauren, Baker, and
Lillian August.

Bountiful
1335 Abbot Kinney Boulevard
Venice, CA 90291
310-450-3620
Nineteenth-century American
painted furniture, European
decor, French lavender soaps,
ribbon-wrapped linens, leather
chairs, and Italian chandeliers.
Full design services available.

The Butera Home Collection
1745 Westcliff Drive
Newport Beach, CA 92660
949-650-8570

1164 South Robertson
    Boulevard
Los Angeles, CA 90035
310-273-4515

Designer furniture and accessories, along with their own
exclusive line of upholstered
furniture. Interior design
appointments available.

Camps and Cottages
1231 North Coast Highway
Laguna Beach, CA 92651
949-376-8474
"Classic cottage offerings with
new-century energy" include
eclectic furnishings and unique
appointments.

Chelsea Antiques
148 Petaluma Boulevard North
Petaluma, CA 94952
707-763-7686
Decorative antiques, col-
lectibles, architecturals, and
garden items.

East Meets West Antiques
160 North La Brea Avenue
Los Angeles, CA 90036
323-931-0500
Nineteenth-century original
painted furniture; antique textiles, including quilts and rugs;
and pillows made from vintage
fabrics.

F. Dorian, Inc.
370 Hayes Street
San Francisco, CA 94102
415-861-3191
Ethnic domestic antiques.

The Gardener
1836 Fourth Street
Berkeley, CA 94710
510-548-4545
www.thegardener.com
Furniture, tabletop items, gifts,
and decorative accessories for
the garden.

Indigo Seas
123 North Robertson Boulevard
Los Angeles, CA 90048
310-550-8758
This shop is styled as an old-
fashioned bazaar in 1930s Paris.

Jimtown Store
6706 State Highway 128
Healdsburg, CA 95448
707-433-1212
www.jimtown.com
The shelves of this 100-year-old
country store are stocked with
old-fashioned toys and candies,
local products and cheeses,
wines, and eclectic housewares
and oddities. The back of the
store offers an eccentric collection of American antiques,
primitives, and folk art.

Kevin Simon Clothing
1358 Abbot Kinney Boulevard
Venice, CA 90291
310-392-4630
www.kevinsimonclothing.com
Handmade clothing and bridal
gowns.

Kim Fiscus Home
1233 North Coast Highway
Laguna Beach, CA 92651
949-464-9612
www.kimfiscushome.com
A streamlined collection of custom furniture paired with 18th-
century to 1940s European
antiques.

Liz's Antique Hardware
453 South La Brea
Los Angeles, CA 90036
323-939-4403
www.LAHardware.com
Anything and everything to
do with decorative hardware
and lighting. Matching service
available.

Mixed Pickles Antiques
1746 Shattuck Avenue
Berkeley, CA 94709
510-649-1353
Antique home furnishings, collectible glassware, California art
pottery, vintage clothing and
accessories, slipcovers, pillows,
and lampshades.

Nantucket Home Furnishings
127 West Third Street
Chico, CA 95928
530-895-1038
www.nantuckethomefurnish-
ings.com
Distinctive gifts, antique to
contemporary furniture, and
decorative accessories for the
entire home, including soaps
and toiletries, glassware, bedding, rugs, upholstery, wicker
furniture, and designer fabrics.
Design consultations available.

Nest
2300 Fillmore Street
San Francisco, CA 94115
415-292-6199

2340 Polk Street
San Francisco, CA 94109
415-292-6198

Both locations offer a refreshing
mix of chic decorative French
accessories, including Provençal
quilts, linens, tabletop, lounge-
ware, and toys.

Prize
2361 San Pablo Avenue
Berkeley, CA 94702
510-848-1168

1415 Green Street
San Francisco, CA 94109
415-771-7215

Both shops are always filled
with 1920s and '30s furniture,
French chandeliers, vintage
hotel silver, glassware, and ever-
changing collections.

Rituals
756 North La Cienega
      Boulevard
Los Angeles, CA 90069
310-854-0848
Antique, vintage, and reproduction lodge, cabin, and ranch-
style furnishings and accessories.
Specializes in Adirondack and
Arts and Crafts. Also does custom design.

**Rose Bowl Flea Market and
Swap Meet**
Pasadena Rose Bowl
1001 Rose Bowl Drive
Pasadena, CA 91103
323-560-7469
More than 2,200 dealers sell
everything from antiques to
crafts here on the second Sunday of each month.

Sienna
119 Petaluma Boulevard North
Petaluma, CA 94952
707-763-6088
Three levels of romantic
French, English, and Italian furniture and accessories.

Swallow Tail
2217 Polk Street
San Francisco, CA 94109
415-567-1555
www.swallowtailhome.com
Nineteenth- to mid-century
antiques and architectural
salvage.

Tail of the Yak
2632 Ashby Avenue
Berkeley, CA 94705
510-841-9891
Amusing, beautiful, unusual,
and occasionally odd things
from everywhere. Both rare and
charmingly incidental.

Vintage Bank Antiques
101 Petaluma Boulevard North
Petaluma, CA 94952
707-769-3097
This antiques collective has
three floors full of California oil
paintings, fine jewelry, silver,
china, furniture, and other
quality antiques.

Wild Goose Chase
105 West Chapman Avenue
Old Towne Orange
Orange, CA 92866
714-532-6807
www.wildgoosechaseca.com
Antique rural Americana, quilts,
Beacon blankets, pre-1900
antiques, and painted furniture.

COLORADO

Another Time, Another Place
1181 South Street
Louisville, CO 80027
720-890-7700
www.atapantiques.com
This website-only source offers
antique enamelware, toleware,
pottery, majolica, copper, wood-
enware, metalware, and textiles.

David Cook Fine Art
1637 Wazee Street
Denver, CO 80202
303-623-8181
www.davidcookfineamerica-
nart.com
Antique American Indian art
with a great selection of old
Navajo rugs and jewelry, Plains
beadwork, baskets, and pottery.
Also shows fine American
paintings.

Willow Antiques and Gifts
3030 East 2nd Avenue,
  Unit 104
Denver, CO 80206
303-570-6379
Pink, silver, and copper lustre-
ware, American pottery, transferware, Victorian dog
collectibles, vintage chenille,
and Indian/camp blankets.

CONNECTICUT

Bungalow
4 Sconset Square
15 Myrtle Avenue
Westport, CT 06880
203-227-4406
With the feeling of a Parisian
market, this shop is filled to the
rafters with antiques, decorative
accessories, and unusual gifts
and treats for the home.

Dovecote
56 Post Road East
Westport, CT 06880
203-222-7500
www.dovecotewestport.com
Everything to decorate the
home from top to bottom,
including Shabby Chic slipcovers, furniture, designer fabrics,
antiques, art, and photography.

East Meets West Antiques
337 Main Street South
Woodbury, CT 06798
203-263-2626
A large collection of 18th- and
19th-century original painted
furniture and textiles, including
antique quilts and rugs and
custom-made pillows of vintage
fabrics.

The Elemental Garden
259 Main Street South
Woodbury, CT 06798
203-263-6500
www.theelementalgarden.com
Antique garden ornaments and
conservatory furnishings.

Hiden Galleries
481 Canal Street
Stamford, CT 06902
203-323-9090
An association of 175 dealers of
antiques, decorative accessories,
textiles, carpets, oil paintings,
and chandeliers and other lighting, with a concentration on
French and Continental
antiques, all displayed in room
settings.

Ile De France Antiques
267 New Milford Turnpike
Marbledale, CT 06777
860-868-4321
www.iledefranceantiques.com
Decorative accessories—
especially French antiques with
an emphasis on kitchenware.

DELAWARE

Shop of the Four Sisters
517 Atlantic Avenue
Millville, DE 19967
302-541-8110
www.shopofthefoursisters.com
This coastal cottage is open
three days a month, with a new
theme and different refurbished
and revamped antique finds
every month.

DISTRICT OF COLUMBIA

David Bell Antiques
1655 Wisconsin Avenue, NW
Washington, DC 20007
202-965-2355
An elegant Georgetown shop
specializing in American, European, architectural, and garden
antiques and decorative arts.

Marston Luce
1651 Wisconsin Avenue
  Northwest
Washington, DC 20007
202-333-6800
French country furniture and
accessories, plus garden
ornaments.

FLORIDA

Sam's Treasure Chest
518 Fleming Street
Key West, FL 33040
305-296-5907
Antiques and collectibles.

Woody Straub Antiques & Art
49 Blue Crab Lane
Panacea, FL 32346
850-349-9788
www.straubart.com
Pre-1940 American Regionalist
art and American country and
period furniture.

GEORGIA

A. Tyner Antiques
200 Bennett Street
Atlanta, GA 30309
404-367-4484
www.swedishantiques.biz
Swedish furniture, including
Gustavian and Biedermeier, and
smalls such as transferware,
herbariums, and leather books.

Antiques in Old Town
93 Main Street
Lilburn, GA 30047
770-279-1300
Housed in a turn-of-the-
century dry goods store, this
unique shop features Victorian,
vintage, country, cottage, and
seasonal antiques and treasures.

Interiors Market
55 Bennett Street NW
Atlanta, GA 30309
404-352-0055

Interiors Market II
200 Bennett Street NW
Atlanta, GA 30309
404-352-0300

www.interiorsmarket.com
Two locations provide more
than 20,000 square feet and
100 dealers of antiques and decorative accessories, including
English and Continental European styles.

Levison & Cullen Gallery
2300 Peachtree Road,
    Suite B-205
Atlanta, GA 30309
404-351-3435
American antiques and decorative art from the 18th and 19th
centuries.

Millie Huckabay American Country Antiques
160 Crowe Road
Alpharetta, GA 30004
770-343-8191
Eighteenth- and 19th-century
lighting, textiles, smalls, American country furniture in original paint surfaces, early toys,
and yellowware.

Romantic Rooms
1502 B Dug Gap Road
Dalton, GA 30720
706-275-0097
European antiques with a lovely
shabby-chic quality.

The Stalls
116 Bennett Street
Atlanta, GA 30309
404-352-4430
www.thestalls.com
Sixty dealers of all types of
antiques and collectibles.

IDAHO

WaterLemon
405 Railroad Avenue
McCall, ID 83638
208-634-2529
American country antiques.
Interior design services
available.

ILLINOIS

Brooke James
1460 North Milwaukee Avenue
Chicago, IL 60622
773-252-4620
www.brookejames.com
This all-white shop is filled with
a mixture of French and
Swedish country antiques,
including rustic furniture.

Joanne Boardman Antiques
522 Joanne Lane
DeKalb, IL 60015
815-756-9359
New England painted furniture
and country accessories.

Mad Parade
1020 West Adams
Chicago, IL 60607
312-738-2680
Nineteenth- and 20th-century
anonymous objects that share a
strong graphic or sculptural ele-
ment, traditional to edgy folk
art, and Americana.

INDIANA

Indianapolis Downtown Antiques Mall
1044 Virginia Avenue
Indianapolis, IN 46203
317-635-5336
Forty dealers offer antique furniture, Depression glass, American art pottery, blue-and-white
stoneware, and other antiques.

Webb's Antique Mall
200 West Union Street
Centerville, IN 47330
765-855-5551
More than 500 dealers of eclectic antiques and collectibles.

IOWA

The Brass Armadillo
701 Northeast 50th Avenue
Des Moines, IA 50313
515-262-0092
This antiques mall houses 400
dealers of antiques and collectibles in its 36,000-square-
foot space.

Especially Lace
202 5th Street
West Des Moines, IA 50265
515-277-9778
A charming collection of vintage lace and linens, antiques, custom lace curtains, April Cornell linens and clothes, unique jewelry, and gifts.

Majestic Lion Antique Center
5048 2nd Avenue
Des Moines, IA 50313
515-282-5466
An antiques mall with 250 dealers offering a variety of antiques and collectibles.

KANSAS

C.S. Post & Co.
117 West 11th Street
Hays, KS 67601
888-419-2399
785-628-3000
www.CSPost.com
This 21st-century version of a general store offers antiques and new home furnishings, including furniture, linens, and kitchen essentials.

LOUISIANA

Antiques for Everyone
Inside the Sports Mall
7288 Greenwood Road
Shreveport, LA 71119
318-938-9903
A large selection of kitchen collectibles, buttons, garden treasures, toys, pottery, glass, paper collectibles, sports collectibles, postcards, and furniture.

Bush Antiques
2109 Magazine Street
New Orleans, LA 70130
504-581-3518
www.bushantiques.com
More than 100 antique beds, religious artifacts, unusual continental furniture, architecturals, and lighting. An eclectic mix with a charming New Orleans flavor.

Lucullus
610 Chartres Street
New Orleans, LA 70130
504-528-9620

3932 Magazine Street
New Orleans, LA 70015
504-894-0500

Both locations specialize in the art of the table and offer everything for eating, dining, and imbibing.

Mac Maison, Ltd.
3963 Magazine Street
New Orleans, LA 70015
504-891-2863
Antiques, architectural artifacts, lighting, and ornamentations.

Mario Villa Gallery
3908 Magazine Street
New Orleans, LA 70115
504-895-8731
www.mariovillagallery.com
High-end art, as well as custom home furnishings, including beds and lighting fixtures.

Wirthmore Antiques
3727 Magazine Street
New Orleans, LA 70015
504-269-0660

3900 Magazine Street
New Orleans, LA 70015
504-899-3811

www.wirthmoreantiques.com
Both locations capture the heartbeat of France with antique furniture, faience pottery, tableware, linens, architectural pieces, fabrics, and more.

MAINE

Dunne Roman
428 Fore Street
Portland, ME 04101
207-780-6456
www.dunneroman.com
Eclectic home furnishings, European soaps, fresh and dried flowers, and gifts and accents.

The Marston House
101 Main Street at Middle
PO Box 517
Wiscasset, ME 04578
207-882-6010
www.marstonhouse.com
Primarily late 18th- and 19th-century American, French, and English painted furniture and accessories, textiles, and garden antiques.

MASSACHUSETTS

G.K.S. Bush, Inc.
13 Old South Road
Nantucket, MA 02554
508-325-0300
Antiques and works of art.

The J. Butler Collection
36 Centre Street
Nantucket, MA 02554
508-228-8429
Each season a new collection
of antiques, fine furniture,
decorative accessories, and
custom-designed items from
throughout the world.

Nantucket Country
38 Centre Street
Nantucket, MA 02554
888-411-8868
American country antiques and
folk art with a specialty in vintage quilts.

Nantucket Looms
16 Main Street
PO Box 1510
Nantucket, MA 02554
508-228-1908
www.nantucketlooms.com
An eclectic assortment of fine
gifts and hand-woven items for
the home and garden.

Seeds Housewares
34 Railroad Street
Great Barrington, MA 01230
413-528-8122
Timeless design in a contemporary setting.

Weeds
14 Centre Street
Nantucket, MA 02554
508-228-5200
www.weeds-nantucket.com
English and French antiques,
nautical and garden antiques,
gifts, exotic shells, hotel silver,
cookware, cachepots, and tins.
Decorator services also
available.

MICHIGAN

Knightsbridge Antiques Mall
42305 West 7 Mile Road
Northville, MI 48167
248-344-7200
More than 200 dealers of
antiques and collectibles.

Marco Polo
13630 Red Arrow Highway
Harbert, MI 49115
269-469-6272
American country pieces as well
as European provincial antiques
with a focus on vintage paint,
lighting, and unusual objects.

MINNESOTA

Junk Market
2460 West Industrial Boulevard
Long Lake, MN 55356
952-249-9151
www.junkmarketonline.com
Junk-style design and lifestyle
experts offer occasional on-site
sales of restored vintage
antiques, including weathered
furniture, architectural salvage,
linens, and garden ornaments.

MISSOURI

Annie Laurie's Antiques
536 Broadway
Cape Girardeau, MO 63701
573-339-1301
This two-story Victorian house
is filled with antiques and rural
ware collected by 50 dealers.

**Apple Wagon Antique Mall
and Home Decor Center**
8509 Old Highway 40
I-70 Exit 155
Williamsburg, MO 63388
573-642-4888
www.applewagon.com
Three stores in one includes a
10,000-square-foot antique
mall, a 6,000-square-foot home
decor center, and a 3,000-
square-foot flea market.

The Curious Sofa
329 Southwest Boulevard
Kansas City, MO 64108
816-221-6600
www.curioussofa.com
Slipcovered furniture, antiques,
Shabby Chic products, French
soap, candles, and jewelry.

NEBRASKA

Olde Glory Antiques
17th Street Shops
1617 South 17th Street
Lincoln, NE 68502
402-474-5679
Historic patriotic antiques and
primitives, painted pieces, holiday items, linens, and sporting
goods.

NEW HAMPSHIRE

The Architectural Attic
49 Center Street
Wolfeboro Falls, NH 03894
603-569-8989
www.architecturalattic.com
Unique home furnishings from
porch posts to teacups, painted
and custom furniture, original
folk art, vintage lighting and
hardware, and architectural and
garden accents.

NEW JERSEY

Amy Karyn Outlet for the Home
48 Coryell Street
Lambertville, NJ 08530
609-397-3075
A wide array of furniture, bedding, pillows, and accessories created with Amy's unique hand-printed fabrics. Antiques and fine collectibles add to the old-world charm.

Point Pleasant Antique Emporium
Bay and Trenton Avenue
Point Pleasant Beach, NJ 08742
800-322-8002
This large antiques mall houses 125 dealers.

NEW MEXICO

The Ann Lawrence Collection
805 Early Street, Suite D
Santa Fe, NM 87501
505-982-1755
Heirloom lace, linens, clothing, decorative objects, and bridal, tribal, and ethnic textiles.

Back at the Ranch
209 East Marcy Street
Santa Fe, NM 87501
800-96BOOTS
www.backattheranch.com
More than 800 pairs of handmade cowboy boots, along with silver jewelry, vintage blanket coats, and buckles.

Barbara Simpson, Inc.
The Design Center
418 Cerrillos Road, Suite 10
Santa Fe, NM 87501
505-983-3314
Vintage folk art and pottery from Mexico, primitives, American folk art, and antique garden and decorative items.

Cowboys & Indians Antiques, Inc.
4000 Central Avenue Southeast
Albuquerque, NM 87108
505-255-4054
www.cowboysandindiansnm.com
Pre-1940s western, folk, and American Indian art and artifacts.

Faircloth and Adams
211 Old Santa Fe Trail
Santa Fe, NM 87501
505-982-8700
Antique furniture, textiles, baskets, folk art, and accessories.

Foxglove
260 Hyde Park Road
Santa Fe, NM 87501
505-986-8285
French, Italian, and English country antique furnishings and architectural and garden elements.

Gloria List Gallery
The Design Center #7
418 Cerrillos Road
Santa Fe, NM 87501
505-982-5622
Seventeenth, 18th-, and 19th-century devotional art from South America, Italy, France, and Mexico.

Lane Coulter Antiques
2120 Conejo Drive
Santa Fe, NM 87505
505-984-8672
Early Navajo jewelry and weavings, New Mexican tinwork, santos, and furniture from the 1850s to 1950.

Nathalie
503 Canyon Road
Santa Fe, NM 87501
800-296-6093
505-982-1021
www.nathaliesantafe.com
An exquisite collection of distinctive high-end western and European clothing, jewelry, and accessories for men, women, and children.

Poem
Sena Plaza Courtyard
125 East Palace Avenue,
　 No. 30
Santa Fe, NM 87501
505-820-7884
Stationery, paper notions, and ephemera, much with a vintage feel. Also carries small decorative items for the home.

Pueblo of Tesque Flea Market
Highway 285, approximately
　 7 miles north of Santa Fe
505-983-2667
505-660-8948
This flea market deals most Fridays, Saturdays, and Sundays May through September and is open Saturdays and Sundays during March and April.

Recollections
530 South Guadalupe Street
Santa Fe, NM 87501
505-988-4775
A consignment shop of fine
antiques, furnishings, and accessories, owned by designer Jane
Smith.

Rio Bravo Trading Company
411 South Guadalupe Street
Santa Fe, NM 87501
505-982-0230
This shop buys, sells, and trades
cowboy and Indian art.

**Todos Santos Chocolates &
Confections**
Sena Plaza Courtyard
125 East Palace Avenue,
    No. 31
Santa Fe, NM 87501
505-982-3855
An eclectic confectionery specializing in chocolate milagros
and saints.

**Wiseman & Gale & Duncan
Interiors Inc.**
150 S. Saint Francis Drive
Santa Fe, NM 87501
505-984-8544
www.wgdinteriors.com
The largest fabric and catalog
library in New Mexico, with a
wonderful collection of antiques
from all over the world, decorative accessories, and fine upholstered furniture. Design services
available.

NEW YORK

ABC Carpet and Home
888 Broadway
New York, NY 10003
212-473-3000
www.abchome.com
Located in a landmark building,
this large store provides seven
floors of rugs, furniture,
antiques, home textiles, accessories, fabrics, and food.

Aero
132 Spring Street
New York, NY 10012
212-966-1500
www.aerostudios.com
An eclectic mix of vintage furniture and furnishings, with new
products for the home as well as
a line of furniture, lamps, and
trays designed by AERO/
Thomas O'Brien.

Aix
462 Broome Street
New York, NY 10013
212-941-7919
French and modern antiques,
plus custom sofas.

The American Wing
2415 Montauk Highway
Bridgehampton, NY 11932
631-537-3319
Vintage rattan, wicker, and
bamboo; American and Continental furniture; small lamps
and lighting; mirrors; and architectural and garden treasures.

Amy Perlin Antiques
306 East 61st Street
New York, NY 10021
212-593-5756
An eclectic collection of 17th-
and 18th-century furniture and
objects.

Anne Moore
2468 Main Street
PO Box 1108
Bridgehampton, NY 11932
631-537-8476
www.annemoore.com
This small hat shop caters to
women, men, and little girls,
with hundreds of hats to choose
from.

Bagley Home
34 Main Street
Sag Harbor, NY 11963
631-725-3553
A tiny shop filled with vintage
French linens, silver cutlery,
antique candlesticks, white
ironstone, and painted country
primitives.

Barbara Trujillo Antiques
2466 Main Street
Bridgehampton, NY 11932
631-537-3838
American country primitives,
holiday-themed antiques, and
Mexican and Indian jewelry.

Basic French
5 East Market Street
Red Hook, NY 12571
845-758-0399
www.basicfrenchonline.com
French lifestyle products for the
home, including soaps, vintage
linens, yellowware, stationery,
children's and adult pajamas,
toys, and religious relics.

Beach Bungalow
26 Main Street
PO Box 2529
Sag Harbor, NY 11963
631-725-4292
Seashore-style home furnishings, including antique and new decorative accessories and furniture, lighting, linens, and interesting shell items.

Bittersweet Interiors
2442 Main Street
Bridgehampton, NY 11932
631-537-5400
www.bittersweetinteriors.com
An eclectic collection of antique French, English, and Scandinavian furniture, architectural and garden ornaments, and unusual accessories, plus custom upholstery. Interior design service available.

Bloom
Sage & Madison Street
Sag Harbor, NY 11963
631-725-5940
Antique and new items for the home and garden.

Chez Soi at Frederick P. Victoria and Son Inc.
2426 Main Street
PO Box 3046
Bridgehampton, NY 11932
631-537-0496
www.dir-dd.com/victoria.html
Furniture and accessories dating from 1740 to 1940.

Davis Pottery
6927 County Highway 18
Unadilla Forks
West Winfield, NY 13491
315-855-4274
www.davispottery.com
Handmade, hand-decorated pottery, terra-cotta gardenware, and antiques.

Distant Origin
153 Mercer Street
New York, NY 10012
212-941-0024
www.distantorigin.com
An eclectic mix of antiques, mirrors, shell art, and accessories.

English Country Antiques
Snake Hollow Road
Bridgehampton, NY 11932
631-537-0606
www.thecatalogues.com
English country antiques, including furniture, china, and baskets; French, Chinese, and European furniture; and new upholstery, linens, and accessories.

Fern
554 Warren Street
Hudson, NY 12534
518-828-2886
Eccentric found objects and furniture from primitive to industrial and architectural.

Gray Gardens
Montauk Highway and
   Poxabogue Lane
Bridgehampton, NY 11932
631-537-4848
A varied mix of American art, early-20th-century furniture, and accessories.

Hammertown Barn
3201 Route 199
Pine Plains, NY 12567
518-398-7075
www.hammertown.com
This original of three shops, located in a 150-year-old barn, offers 19th-century English and American antiques, rugs, lighting, fine gifts, and home furnishings. Other locations in Rhinebeck, New York, and Great Barrington, Massachusetts.

Interieurs
151 Franklin Street
New York, NY 10013
212-343-0800
High-end French modern furniture combined with unique handcrafted furniture, accessories, and antiques.

John Derian Company Inc.
6 East Second Street
New York, NY 10003
212-677-3917
www.johnderian.com
An emporium of handmade decorative decoupaged accessories, antiques, and imports.

Judith and James Milne, Inc.
506 East 74th Street
New York, NY 10021
212-472-0107
www.milneantiques.com
American country antiques and folk art.

Kate's Paperie
561 Broadway
New York, NY 10012
212-941-9816
www.katespaperie.com
More than 4,000 exotic papers
and more than 1,500 types of
ribbon, as well as fine stationery, photo albums, and
journals.

Kelter Malcé Antiques
74 Jane Street
New York, NY 10014
212-675-7380

2466 Main Street
Bridgehampton, NY 11932
631-537-3838

American folk art, painted furniture, quilts, rugs, early textiles, Native American arts, and
amusing eccentricities.

Kinneman & Ramaekers
2466 Main Street
Bridgehampton, NY 11932
631-537-3838
Fine American antiques.

**Laura Fisher Antique Quilts &
Americana**
1050 Second Avenue
New York, NY 10022
212-838-2596
This gallery shop is the source
for antique quilts, hooked rugs,
and other textiles.

Liza Sherman Antiques
112 Hampton Street
Sag Harbor, NY 11963
631-725-1437

19 West 55th Street, Suite 6A
New York, NY 10019
212-581-1925

Both locations offer unusual
and offbeat sculpture, accessories, textile art, ornamental
stones, and Napoleon III
chaises.

Mecox Gardens
257 County Road 39A
Southampton, NY 11968
631-287-5015
www.mecoxgardens.com
Antique garden ornaments,
unusual home furnishings and
accessories, and architectural
plants, pottery, and urns.

Melet Mercantile
84 Wooster Street, Suite 205
New York, NY 10012
212-925-8353
This showroom offers antique
textiles, vintage clothing, jewelry, watches, and other cool
stuff all fused together in a
lifestyle format. By appointment only.

Privet Cove
69 Jobs Lane
Southampton, NY 11968
631-287-5685
www.privetcove.com
Large nautilus shells, mermaid
prints, sterling and precious
stone jewelry, reproduction
whiteware, vintage pottery, and
their own line of teak furniture.

Sage Street Antiques
Corner of Rt. 114 and Sage
    Street
Sag Harbor, NY 11963
631-725-4036
A weekends-only shop that sells
country antiques, kitchen
kitsch, and framed antique
prints, as well as many treasures
at yard-sale prices.

Takashimaya New York
693 Fifth Avenue
New York, NY 10022
212-350-0100
Seven floors of aesthetic elements from around the globe,
including tabletop items, decorative accessories, bedding,
clothing, bath and beauty essentials, and flowers.

Treillage Ltd.
418 East 75th Street
New York, NY 10021
212-535-2288
www.treillageonline.com
This upscale shop specializes in
garden antiques.

NORTH CAROLINA

The Farmer's Wife
339 South Davie Street
Greensboro, NC 27401
336-274-7920
Mantels and other architectural
antiques, garden-related collectibles and vintage prints, and
simple-lined furniture and
accessories. Fresh flowers also
available.

Summerhouse
1722 Battleground Avenue
Greensboro, NC 27408
336-275-9655
www.summerhousestore.com
Vintage and cottage-style treasures such as slipcovered sofas, old wicker, painted primitive cupboards, lamps, garden pieces, transferware, linens, and soaps.

OHIO

America Antiques and Emporium
26 South Third Street
Newark, OH 43055
740-345-0588
Three floors of American primitives as well as cottage and home concepts.

Marjorie Staufer
2244 Remsen Road
Medina, OH 44256
330-239-1443
American 18th- and 19th-century furniture and smalls in original paints and finishes. By appointment only.

OKLAHOMA

Grandma Had It Antiques and Gifts
36700 Old Highway 270
Shawnee, OK 74804
405-275-7766
Three buildings of quilts, primitives, painted furniture, glass, lawn and garden iron, French and Victorian antiques, and seasonal items.

Sampler Antiques
9201 North Western Avenue
Oklahoma City, OK 73114
405-848-7007
Americana, primitives, and lodge collectibles.

OREGON

Circa AD
1204 Glisan Street
Portland, OR 97209
503-221-1269
Carefully selected 19th-century painted pieces, farmhouse furnishings, garden ornaments, and home accessories from Europe.

Pacific Cottage
726 Pacific Way
PO Box 2443
Gearhart, OR 97138
503-738-6560
800-738-6560
www.pacificcottage.com
Cottage-style home decor, including antiques, French soaps and lotions, folk art, Cath Kidston linens, and accessories.

Stars Antique Mall
7027 Southeast Milwaukie
   Avenue
Portland, OR 97202
503-239-0346

. . . More Stars
6717 Southeast Milwaukie
   Avenue
Portland, OR 97202
503-239-3142
www.StarsAntique.com
This 10,000-square-foot antiques malls carry antiques, collectibles, and extraordinary junk.

PENNSYLVANIA

Hoffman Woodward
412 West King Street
East Berlin, PA 17316
717-259-7676
www.hoffmanwoodward.com
Painted furniture and accoutrements for the period home and garden.

TENNESSEE

Heart of Country Antiques Show
www.heartofcountry.com
Held at Nashville's Gaylord Opryland Resort in February and October, this antiques show offers the best in country primitives, Americana, folk art, textiles, painted furniture, lighting, pottery, and more.
For more information, contact
Richard E. Kramer & Associates
427 Midvale Avenue
St. Louis, MO 63130
800-862-1090

Joy Haley Antiques
102 Brighton Close
Nashville, TN 37205
615-297-6364
High-end country furniture and accessories, plus upscale leather floor mats by Idlewild Design.

TEXAS

The Antique Pavilion
2311 Westheimer
Houston, TX 77098
713-520-9755
An antiques mall with European and American 18th- and 19th-century furniture, accessories, china, glassware, silver, and jewelry.

Brian Stringer Antiques
2031 West Alabama
Houston, TX 77098
713-526-7380
English and European
antiques and accessories and
reproductions.

Ceylon et Cie
1500 Market Center Boulevard
Dallas, TX 75207
214-742-7632
www.ceylonetcie.com
Eighteenth, 19th-, and 20th-
century French, Italian, and
Indian antiques, unusual accessories, architecturals, and textiles. Custom furniture and
design services available.

**Emma Lee Turney's Round
Top Antiques Fair**
PO Box 821289
Houston, TX 77282
281-493-5501
www.roundtopantiquesfair.com
For the first weekend of April
and October, four locations in
Round Top, Texas, are filled
with the best of country
antiques and folk art.

The Gray Door
1809 West Gray
Houston, TX 77019
713-521-9085
A charming collection of hand-
selected singular pieces from
Scandinavia, the United King-
dom, and the Continent,
including 18th- through 20th-
century furniture, art, lighting,
and accessories.

Hot Tamale Antiques
PO Box 930
Aledo, TX 76008
817-291-3952
www.hot-tamale-antiques.com
American antique textiles, folk
art, furniture, quilts, lighting,
hooked rugs, baskets, floral textiles, and western antiques.

Indulge
2700 West Alabama
Houston, TX 77098
713-888-0181
An apothecary for the soul
known for specialty orchids and
European bath products.

Jane Moore Interiors
2922 Virginia
Houston, TX 77098
713-526-6113
Eighteenth- and 19th-century
decorations and antiques from
France, England, and Sweden.
Also offers interior design
services.

Judith McClellan
1003 West 34th Street, Suite D
Houston, TX 77018
713-880-9449
www.judithmcclellan.com
This direct importer of antiques
from Europe and Asia also
houses one of the largest collections of vintage linens in
America.

Karen Sobotka
The Antique Pavilion
3407 Tangley Street
Houston, TX 77055
713-664-3972
An eclectic mix of antique furniture, textiles, and decorative
goods.

**Kay O'Toole Antiques and
Eccentricities**
1921 Westheimer
Houston, TX 77098
713-523-1921
French and Italian furniture,
decorative and architectural
items, chandeliers and sconces,
antique fabrics, and screens.

Lovers Lane Antique Market
5001 West Lovers Lane
Dallas, TX 75209
214-351-5656
www.loverslaneantiques.com
Thirty different antiques shops.

Rocketbuster Boots
115 South Anthony Street
El Paso, TX 79901
915-541-1300
www.rocketbuster.com
Handmade vintage-style boots
and leather goods.

Room Service by Ann Fox
4354 Lovers Lane
Dallas, TX 75225
214-369-7666
www.roomservicehome.com
This cottage-style shop offers a
great selection of vintage and
reproduction painted furniture,
in-stock fabrics, bedding, and
gifts.

Rue No. 1
6701 Snider Plaza
Dallas, TX 75205
214-265-0900
A French-influenced home store
filled with vintage finds from
French flea markets.

Shabby Slips
2304 Bissonnet
Houston, TX 77005
713-630-0066
Custom furniture and imported
European antiques.

**The Sitting Room/Ginger
Barber Design Inc.**
2121 Woodhead
Houston, TX 77019
713-523-1932
www.thesittingroom.net
Real room settings filled with
new and vintage garden-style
furniture and accessories,
including natural-fiber upholstery, European antiques, dried
topiaries, wicker baskets, and
unusual lamps.

Uncommon Objects
1512 South Congress Avenue
Austin, TX 78704
512-442-4000
An incredible collection of
antiques, oddities, and curious
goods from all over the place.

**Watkins Culver Gardner
Antiques-Design**
2308 Bissonnet Street
Houston, TX 77005
713-529-0597
Eighteenth- and 19th-century
furnishings and accessories with
distinctive style.

UTAH

The Butera Home Collection
255 Heber Avenue
Park City, UT 84060
435-649-5540
Designer furniture and accessories and their own exclusive
line of upholstered furniture.
Interior design services
available.

Cats Cradle
168 West Center Street
Provo, UT 84605
801-374-1832
"Arty eclectica," including folk
art, vintage holiday items, religious pieces, and finds from
closed-down shops, toy stores,
and factories.

VERMONT

**Judy Pascal Antiques &
Interiors**
at Le Dépot
Elm Street
Manchester Center,
    VT 05255
802-362-2004
Country furnishings, garden
accents, painted furniture, vintage textiles, and architecturals.

VIRGINIA

Old Lucketts Store
42350 Lucketts Road
Leesburg, VA 20176
703-779-0268
This 6,000-square-foot shop is
packed with great finds, including primitives and garden
accents.

Sisters Maison Unique
116 South Royal Street
Alexandria, VA 22314
703-683-7533
Gifts and home accessories with
a French theme.

WASHINGTON

La Campagne
1569 Northfork Road
Chehalis, WA 98532
360-262-3538
Three buildings full of American and Continental country-
style furnishings and original
one-of-a-kind merchandise,
including beds and linens, furniture, antique jewelry, lamps,
and topiaries.

Nest Feathers
301 Wellsian Way
Richland, WA 99352
509-943-3374
www.nestfeathers.com
Cottage-style furnishings and
accessories, especially painted
furniture.

WISCONSIN

Blackberry Road Antiques
12547 Blackberry Road
Ellison Bay, WI 54210
920-854-7846
A barn-turned-shop filled with
antique furniture, architectural
salvage, and vintage garden
accessories.

Index

17/12